Starting Out Together
a book for those considering marriage

Gavin Reid

HODDER AND STOUGHTON
LONDON SYDNEY AUCKLAND TORONTO

For Mamie
whose marriage with Harvey
was an inspiration to
many of us

British Library Cataloguing in Publication Data

Reid, Gavin
    Starting out together.
    1. Marriage
    I. Title
    301.42   HQ734

ISBN 0 340 26567 1

ABOUT THIS BOOK

When my publisher – God bless him – suggested that I write a book about getting married I showed the letter to my wife and we both laughed. Who were we to set out to tell others about marriage?

Later the same morning as I thought about it I decided to 'have a go' all the same. Mary and I could never claim to be the perfect married couple. We have made mistakes and I went pretty close to wrecking the marriage at one stage. On the other hand, after twenty years of living as man and wife we can only thank God for thinking up the idea! And at the heart of this book is my conviction that in marriage we are going over a course that a loving Creator has planned.

At the end of the day that is why marriage is important.

This book is for those who have just got engaged or who are thinking about it pretty seriously. I have tried to keep the stars out of my eyes in writing it because marriage needs some pretty honest and realistic thinking from square one, if it is to prove the liberating and joyous adventure it is meant to be.

I have also tried to remember where so many young people actually *are*. I shall probably be criticised by some because I talk gently to those who have had sexual experience before marriage. The fact is that many young people are in this boat. If I were to pretend that sex-before-marriage did not exist, I would not be able to help a great many readers.

On the other hand, I shall also be criticised as being hopelessly old-fashioned and narrow because I make no secret of my view that sex outside of marriage is wrong. However, I must be true to myself and – more important still – I must be true to God. The truth I believe is that God is against this behaviour because it is against our own best interests. The condemnation of God comes out of his amazing love for us. He hates to see us spoiling our lives and the world around us.

Some readers might be surprised that I, a Christian minister, have used so much space in this book to talk about practical matters. My answer is that marriage is a very practical business. Others may even be disgusted that I actually talk about sex. My answer to that is that sex was God's idea in the first place and if they do not approve of it they should write to him!

I would like to thank Pam Barden for typing most of this book and also Dr. George Hobbs, Michael Barnes and Alaric Hurst for valuable advice on practical matters. All mistakes, however, are my own fault! Thanks are also due to 'Taffy' for his excellent cartoons.

Finally for all young lovers who may be reading these words I have this to say: *God Bless you. Take marriage seriously but never let it be serious!*

GAVIN REID

CONTENTS

CHAPTER 1

'WHAT ARE WE LETTING OURSELVES IN FOR?'

'Congratulations!' they all say.

You have just announced your engagement and everyone starts grinning fiercely and treating you as if you had just broken a world record! And yet at the same time the joking starts about 'settling down' and the end of freedom.

So what is the truth? There are some today who pour scorn upon formal marriage and call the certificate a there 'scrap of paper' that isn't necessary. Popular newspapers are not short of reports about people in the public eye who 'live together' outside of marriage and claim that such a way gives more freedom. Have they got a point?

And then again all around us we hear of marriages breaking down. One out of every five marriages ends in a divorce court. Would it not be less painful to avoid getting married altogether?

And yet marriage is still popular. Opinion polls have shown that about eighty-five per cent of today's young people think that marriage is a good thing. And they are right. I would go further. I would suggest that outside of discovering the reality of God, marriage can be the greatest thing that happens to a man or woman. There is no round-the-world voyage or mountaineering expedition that can match the sheer adventure of a man and a woman journeying into the future determined to love each other in the bad times as well as the good, 'in sickness and in health'.

Very few of us are gifted enough to be great painters, sculptors or musicians. But marriage gives us a chance to create a work of art. The raw materials are two self-centred people. The end product can be a oneness and harmony, not only between the two but also within the home and family that they have created. To do this is to put together a work of art that makes the stuff in art galleries look like a child's scribblings!

So what is marriage all about? Here are four things that the Bible says about marriage.

1. TOGETHERNESS

Right at the beginning of the Bible is the story of the Garden of Eden. There are many today who would write this off as a sort of fairy tale, which is a great pity because it means they do not see the message behind it.

In the story we read that when he had created one of the sexes – the man – God our Creator says: 'It is not good for the man to live alone', and so the woman is created. Togetherness and companionship are at the heart of marriage. The basic unit of the human race is not a solo human being but rather the married couple supporting and helping each other. And the more you study the human being compared with the animals, the more you see the need for this togetherness. Unlike some species, the human child takes a long time to grow up and it is obvious that his or her parents need to stick together to protect the growing child and to prepare it for adult life.

Again there are tremendous differences in the way men and women have been created. They are not only physically different, they are emotionally different. The qualities of a man need to be balanced by the qualities of a woman. Take away one or the other sex and we only see half of what humanity is about. We need each other – togetherness is built into mankind.

2. COMMITMENT

There is a moment in the launching of a rocket when the whole process of the count-down has passed the point of no return. In the televised launchings from Cape Canaveral one got used to hearing the ground controller's voice saying, *'We have commit!'*

Marriage is about two people getting past the point of no return with regard to the coming together of their lives. They 'have commit'. Now this is not to be confused with what is popularly called 'falling in love'. Popular songs can often give the idea that our wills and minds play little or no part. People fall in love – we are told – get married and live happily ever after.

It isn't like that at all. Such a view is a very childish and unrealistic one. Feelings of being head-over-heels in love with someone are grand and we should enjoy them to the full, but marriage is made of sterner stuff. In the wedding service we are not asked: 'Are you in love' with the other person? We are not even asked: 'Do you love' the other person? We are asked: *'Will you love?'*

Marriage is about our *wills*. It is about making up our *minds* and promising to keep our word on the matter of love and loyalty. Commitment does not end when we stop feeling loving. When I hear people talking about divorce because 'they are no longer in love', I believe what they are really saying is that they never understood what marriage was about in the first place.

All this may sound very unromantic but it happens to be important and realistic. Many a marriage has been rescued and brought back to being a happy one because the partners refused to give up on each other when they hit the bad times and when their *feelings* of love had gone. Marriage itself, or the person we marry, is not like some toy that we throw away for another when we get bored with it.

That is why it is so important to take great care about who we marry. I once heard someone say that the problem was not that divorce was too easy to come by, it was rather that marriage was too easy to enter into. Good looks and charm are not enough. Sex appeal is all very well but married people spend far more of their lives out of bed than in it! We should not ask ourselves whether the other person 'turns us on'. The big question is – *can we see each other living in the closest possible way for the rest our lives?*

Secure marriages, and because of them secure families,

12

are the basic 'bricks' from which a stable society is built. That's why marriages can never be private affairs and why they must be publicly recognised and respected. Ordered society is about people committing themselves to live alongside each other. If the basic unit of man and wife is weak then the whole building is in danger of collapse.

3. SEXUAL FULFILMENT

All this stuff about commitment may sound very solemn, and so it is. But marriage is meant to be fun! God has given human beings a far greater amount of sexual desire than any other species. And if God has given us this tremendous sexual appetite he expects us to express it. The important thing is that our sexual powers are used in the right way. And marriage – the pledged, deliberately-willed partnership of a man and a woman – is the right way.

Sex is fun. Sex is thrilling. Sex enriches life. Everybody knows that. What is often overlooked, however, is that sexual intercourse is a very profound, life-changing experience. It creates something permanent between the people who take part. I believe it is impossible for two people to experience total spiritual and emotional satisfaction within intercourse if there is no intention of staying together afterwards. The sexual union is the ultimate giving of oneself to the other person. And an ultimate relationship like this cannot be shared with more than one person.

Now I am well aware that some – probably many – reading these words will already have had sexual experience outside of marriage. To such people two things need to be said.

First, sex outside marriage is always less than the best.

13

It is viewed seriously by God because he loves us and wants the best for us and he wants happy marriages and stable societies. But God is the great forgiver and mender of spoiled or broken lives. Further, he knows our weaknesses and our wrongfulness and he also knows the immense pressures that are put upon us in the whole area of sexual awareness. There are far worse sins than sex outside of marriage and the fact that one is not a virgin is no reason for not having a Christian wedding in church if you really desire it.

Second, I believe it is important to be frank with each other before marriage about any previous sexual experience. To discover this later, after marriage, can often deeply hurt the husband or wife. It can even wreck the marriage. If there is real love then there will be understanding and forgiveness. If there isn't such understanding and forgiveness then the sooner one finds out the better!

4. HAVING CHILDREN

Marriage is all about having children. Some think it right to say that this is the first reason for marriage, but this is a mistaken view. Children can be born out of wedlock with the greatest of ease, but this is always tragic. Children need to grow up in homes where the parents find joy in one another. Children need homes where the marriages are recognised by the society in which they live, and where to some degree the marriages are protected and discouraged from breaking up.

If we want stable children we need stable marriages.

But children not only need healthy marriages. Healthy marriages need children. Except for reasons of age I cannot feel that it is right to plan for a marriage without children. They may be expensive and they certainly make for hard work, but the tasks of parenthood draw out the best and most noble in human beings. And the joys are immense. To see your baby taking its first steps; your youngster bravely facing the first day at school; your teenager beginning to show the first signs of responsible adulthood – these are amongst the most profound joys I know. They are worth all the broken nights and the clearing up!

There is an important truth tucked away in here. Love cannot keep itself to itself. A man and woman who love each other will generate more love, and that needs to be shared with others. Children are the first and most obvious area for this shared love. But it must never stop there. In recent years it has become fashionable to criticise the 'nuclear family'. What the critics attack is the self-centredness of so many homes. The old phrase about 'the Englishman's home is his castle' has been all too true – and not just in the case of Englishmen either.

I believe that God's plan is that our homes should be outward-looking. I remember two older friends of mine who had been missionaries in Kenya. There were many lessons they had learned from the Africans amongst whom they had lived. One was this: *their doors were always open*. Their home was always a place of welcome. All our homes should be like that.

So then marriage is about togetherness, commitment, sexual fulfilment and having children. It is the greatest adventure a man or woman can face. Anyone considering marriage should take it seriously. Above all we need to be as sure about each other on our wedding day as it is possible to be.

CHAPTER 2

'ARE WE RIGHT FOR EACH OTHER?'

Before expeditions set out to climb some unconquered mountain the team members are chosen with care. Skills at mountaineering are not enough. The team has to 'gel' – they have to be right for each other. If they are not, then when the pressures come, tempers fray, rivalries come to the surface and the expedition can come to grief.

This is exactly the case with marriage. I have a feeling that failures in a marriage can nearly always be traced back to things that could have been discovered before the wedding day if only we had looked for them. A newly published wedding service which is now being used in many churches gives this warning about marriage:

... it must not be undertaken carelessly, lightly or selfishly, but reverently, responsibly and after serious thought.[1]

All this sounds very serious – but then the best and most important things in life usually are. If marriage is a great adventure then those who set out upon it need to be right for each other.

Of course there is no way of being absolutely certain about this sort of thing. It is one thing to take marriage seriously but it is quite something else for a couple to become so worried about whether they are right for each other that they end up being uncertain of anything. Again, none of us is perfect. If we all start looking for perfect people to marry then nobody is ever going to see a wedding day!

'COURTING'

This business of finding out about each other is what 'courting' is supposed to be about. Unfortunately many couples get too quickly into what I call the 'eyeball to eyeball' stage. Kissing and cuddling is grand, but it doesn't exactly help us to learn very much about each other! If there are irritating or strange sides to our characters then it is better to discover these before the engagement ring is bought.

It has been said that daughters tend to be like their

[1] The Marriage Service – *Alternative Service Book*

mothers and I would add that sons often take after their fathers also. It is worth remembering this when you visit possible future parents-in-law. We also need to be very realistic about our temperaments. If one of a couple is an excitable, 'jumpy', or anxious sort of a person then there could be trouble ahead if the other has a similar temperament. It is usually important for at least one of the partners to be a calm person.

Age differences need thinking about. There have been many happy marriages where the man was up to ten years older than the woman. Marriages when the woman is considerably older than the man are more prone to difficulties. Again when someone is considering marriage to a person considerably older there can sometimes be a hidden reason which needs facing honestly. Is the girl actually looking for a father figure? Is the man looking for a substitute mother? If the answer is 'yes' then there are likely to be serious problems ahead.

EIGHT QUESTIONS

Here are eight questions that every couple thinking about getting married ought to ask themselves.

1. *How long have I known him/her?* Lightning love affairs with people being swept off their feet don't always end up as happy marriages. It usually takes a good deal of time to get to know another person really well. Why rush? We don't learn about each other curled up on the sofa – surprising though this may sound. We learn about each other by going to places together, meeting each other's friends, talking over what we believe about life and what we want out of marriage.

All this takes time – and time is what young people have in plenty!

2. *Am I old enough to know what I want for the rest of my life?* People's bodies mature long before their characters are fully developed and their emotions have settled. It is a sad fact that one in three of all marriages entered into by people under twenty-one ends in divorce. Those in that age group need to be doubly sure before fixing the big day.

3. *Am I marrying him/her because I want to be with him/her – or because I want to get away from someone else?* Not all of us are fortunate enough to come from happy homes or to live in pleasant circumstances. But this should never make us rush into marriage as a way of escape. It is a very hurtful thing for someone to learn that he or she was married only as a means to an end. To marry someone is to say that you want to share that person's life. No other reason is good enough.

4. *Am I marrying him/her for what he/she is or am I hoping to be able to change him/her in the future?* This is an important question which comes right back to whether we love people for what they are in themselves or whether we have a dream person in mind and hope to change our partners to be more like our dreams. Real love – the sort that comes from God himself – accepts us for what we are. Married people need to know that even if they do not change much over the years (and most of us do) they will still be loved.

Sometimes I meet the ambitious wife who tries to push her husband into 'bettering himself'. It rarely works unless the husband wants to do this in any case. I have seen this bring friction and unhappiness into a marriage.

5. *Are we agreed about the standard of living we expect*

after marriage? This is another area that can lead to discontent. The husband is content with a simple lifestyle. He maintains an old car and has little interest in the latest fashions. And all the time the wife wishes that they were keeping up with the Joneses with a bigger house, new car and all the rest. Of course it can be the other way around with the husband becoming a 'high flyer' and wishing his wife would stop settling for being tied to housework.

Now there are bigger questions of right and wrong, selfishness and materialism here, but my concern for the moment is simply to point out that trouble looms ahead for the couple that haven't agreed in advance the sort of life-style they hope to achieve as husband and wife.

6. *Are we agreed about having a family and the number of children (ideally) we would like?* I have met people who didn't discover until after marriage that their partners didn't want children! This sort of thing can lead to great bitterness. As with the previous question there are moral issues at stake, but again my point here is the need for the engaged couple to have an agreed picture of the sort of home and family they would like to see in the days ahead.

7. *Am I marrying a FRIEND?* This may seem an odd question but I believe it is the key to a successful marriage. I would go so far as to say that many couples who get married don't have a particularly deep friendship.

With current thinking stressing the sexual side of life so greatly, simple friendship between the sexes can get forgotten. The impression can be given that we look for people whose looks bowl us over or make us go wobbly-kneed. But this is to reduce human beings to dolls if not to sex-objects.

Of course it doesn't help if we find the other person sexually repulsive, but this is hardly likely! What is important (and I hear too few people saying this) is that we see marriage as lifelong friendship. Most of our married lives are spent out of bed. We are going to grow old and less physically attractive – all of us. To be married successfully calls for trust, interest in each other's affairs, some common interests (although it is good to be able to 'do our own thing' also) and enjoyment of each other's conversation. Very often marriage degenerates to a house-keeping and sex arrangement with the partners living in two different worlds. The husband who looks to 'nights out with the boys' for his fun and to his wife for bed, breakfast and clean shirts is heading for trouble. He will deserve it!

8. *Are we agreed about God?* This may be my last question but it is not an afterthought. I believe it is the most important question of all. To have discovered that Jesus Christ is a living person and that we have a caring heavenly Father, *makes us different people.* A couple can have different views about football and different views about politics and still get along together well. But if one is a committed Christian and the other has no basic sympathy with Christian belief then something that is very precious to one cannot be shared with the other.

And Christianity is far more than head belief. It is a whole way of life. It affects our understanding of true and false, good and bad. I have seen many marriages divided over Christianity, usually because one of the partners became a Christian after marriage. It can be such a strain that there is no way I could commend deliberately setting out on married life with this difference between a couple. In the very early days of Christianity St. Paul gave advice to any Christian woman who had been widowed. 'She is free to be married to any man she wishes,' he wrote. 'But only if he is a Christian.' It seems a harsh teaching but it comes from a concern that people find real togetherness in marriage. It has nothing to do with Christian thinking of themselves as 'superior' in any way.

All this obviously applies to marriage with someone who is committed to another religion like Islam or Buddhism. But what about denominational differences? Here the matter is obviously far less difficult. No denomination has the right to say: 'We are the only real Christians around the place.' Some of us may get close to saying things like that, but we are fools if we do. All who put their trust in God as we have seen him shown and explained in Jesus Christ are Christians. However, there are problems that can become niggles and sadnesses later on if they are not talked through before marriage.

Two such problems come to mind. The first is: What church will we join *as a married couple*? It surely is out of the question to think of splitting up for worship on Sunday. Again it can never be ideal to flit around between two churches all the time. A church is far more than a place you attend. It is a family and every Christian should *belong* to a local church family and take a full part in its life. There needs to be agreement about this and one of the partners has got to give a little. This does not mean that an occasional visit to services of the other denomination (by *both*) would not be a good thing.

The second problem is the upbringing of children. Here the matter is surely decided by the choice of church that the couple have made up their minds to join. It is surely unthinkable to belong to one church and to try to take your children to another.

These problems become a bit sharper and more difficult where one of the partners is a Roman Catholic. In

22

the past the Roman Church has put down strict guidelines affecting the upbringing of children. We live in changing times where a much warmer atmosphere exists between Roman Catholics and Protestants. It is far the best way in this situation for the couple to talk things over both with the Roman Catholic priest and with the minister of the other denomination.

The trouble with a chapter like this is it seems such a wet blanket! Everything is love and kisses all the way and in comes some moaning minnie to pour cold water on everything and make it sound so serious and matter-of-fact.

I'm sorry! The amazing thing about marriage is that it is just this mixture. It *is* love and kisses and romance and rolling around breathless in each other's arms – and praise God for that! And yet it is also a sensible, thought-out contract between two people who have considered what they are doing.

And the important thing to remember is that it is usually those who put most thought into marriage who get most joy out of it.

BEFORE YOU BUY THE RING . . .

A checklist to avoid a broken heart!

1. *Do I want to marry him/her:*
   - (a) Because I want to get away from someone
     else?   YES/NO
   - (b) Because of his/her sex appeal?   YES/NO
   - (c) Because I can make him/her different?   YES/NO
   - (d) Because of his/her money or reputation?   YES/NO
   - (e) Because I'm afraid of being 'left on the
     shelf'?   YES/NO

If you score one 'Yes' or more don't buy the ring –
talk about it!

2. *Do we agree about:*
   (a) Jesus Christ as Lord and Saviour?   YES/NO
   (b) The standard of living and life-style that
       would be right?   YES/NO
   (c) The number of children we would ideally like
       to have?   YES/NO

If you score one 'NO' or more, don't buy the ring –
talk about it!

3. *Do you find him/her:*
   (a) To be a real *friend* as well as a sweetheart? YES/NO
   (b) Someone who makes you feel at peace and
       'safe'?   YES/NO
   (c) Someone you can trust and respect?   YES/NO
   (d) Someone you like your friends and family
       to meet?   YES/NO
   (e) Someone who brings out the best in you? YES/NO
   (f) Someone you would like to be with in a
       crisis?   YES/NO
   (g) Someone you would be happy to live with even
       if he/she became an invalid?   YES/NO

If you score one 'NO' or more don't buy the ring –
talk about it!
If you pass the whole test – why not buy the ring!

reproduced by permission of
Buzz Magazine

CHAPTER 3

VIVE LA DIFFÉRENCE!

You may have just possibly noticed that men and women are different!

The obvious difference is physical. Boys and girls are born looking fairly alike apart from their sex organs. At pram and toddler stage you can hear people asking: 'Is it a boy or a girl?' As they grow older you can still find a young lad with girlish features and tearaway girls playing football with the boys. As we all know, the physical changes begin to show themselves between ten and fifteen years – sooner with girls than boys. The girls become more shapely and the boys become more rugged, start needing to shave, and their voices break.

WHAT MAKES A WOMAN TICK?

All this we know. What is sometimes not realised is how deep these changes go into our emotions and our awareness. The changes we see in a girl are really the tip of an iceberg. Something very profound is going on and it's a pity that many boys never realise this. Indeed young men can enter marriage (particularly if they grew up without sisters) almost clueless about 'what makes a woman tick'.

At puberty a girl starts having periods. What this means is that her body starts going into action for the job of producing babies. She produces the female cell or egg and every four weeks one unused cell (or cells) is cleared out of the system by a flow of blood and another takes its place. The process of clearing-out is called menstruation and it can be uncomfortable. Quite frankly it can also be a bit messy. Girls soon get used to it and modern sanitary products have worked wonders in keeping everything tidy and allowing girls to live a full and free life during their periods.

The few days just before a period starts can often be a time when the girl feels tense or flat. It's a bad time for her to make decisions. She can look on the gloomy side of life too easily! A few days after the period is over comes the process known as ovulation when the new cell is put in place for possible fertilisation and the conceiving of a child. This also can give rise to a short time of discomfort.

Add to all this the mysterious business of hormones and glands and what you have is this – a woman is always aware that she is a woman and a potential mother. This is something quite different from men. Men can be almost detached from their sexuality. They can almost turn it on and off – not so with women. There is this gentle, continuous awareness of what she is sexually.

MEN CAN BE DETACHED

Men have nothing remotely like the monthly cycle. The nearest is when their production system of male cells (sperms) becomes overloaded and while sleeping they have a 'nocturnal emission' or 'wet dream'. When this happens they ejaculate as they would during normal sexual intercourse. It can prove a little embarrassing at times but it is absolutely normal (and parents or room mates know what it's all about so why worry?).

These nocturnal emissions can often be accompanied by a sexy dream and certainly by a pleasurable sensation. There is nothing wrong with this and sensitive souls should thank God that they are normal! What can happen as a result of this is that a boy discovers sexual pleasure, and in one way or another learns that he can stimulate himself to get the same pleasant sensations. This is called masturbation and usually leads to guilt feelings amongst sensitive youngsters, particularly as one can get 'hooked' on masturbating during the teenage years.

The truth is that it is part of coming to sexual self-awareness and therefore part of growing up. It becomes immature behaviour after a while and it could be a problem with perverted aspects to it if it carries on through to adult life, but this is fairly rare as far as I can see.

My purpose here is not to talk about the rights and wrongs of masturbation. What I want to show is that the dawning of sexual awareness in boys is a much more casual business than it is with girls. And all through life sexual feelings are more quickly aroused and more quickly satisfied in men than in women. In sexual intercourse this is certainly the case. After his orgasm he can often feel tired out and ready to turn away and sleep. For the girl this can be desperately hurtful. She may not have felt any peak of pleasure but rather a deep joy in the togetherness, and to turn it off abruptly jars and even makes her feel that she has just been 'used'.

This deep awareness of being a woman affects courtship and home making. Courtship for the boy can often mean no more than pleasant flirting. For the girl it can often mean an underlying awareness that here is the possible mate, father of children, source of security and central figure for the future.

WHAT A GIRL IS GIVING UP

I do not think many of us menfolk realise what a girl is giving up when she consents to marry. Even in these days with talk of equality and 'women's lib' a girl enters marriage knowing that she will have less freedom of action than her husband. The producing and raising of children is an imprisoning period of one's life which calls for sacrifices. The sheer level of dependence and demand of young children is exhausting. Their very lives depend on their mother's dedication in the early days. Husbands dash off to work – often meeting other women to 'chat up' – they come home expecting meals to be ready, they see no problem in nipping off to evening or weekend activities with their friends; and all the time the mother is holding the home together.

Even when husbands are more considerate than I have described and take their full share of running a home and raising children, the wife and mother can feel the lack of adult company – especially with the opposite sex – and can be aware of what she is no longer free to do or to be. You need a very deep commitment to the role of woman and possible mother to face these prospects, but in my experience that commitment seems to be built in to most young women. It is deeply felt. Love, marriage, home and family are all part of the average normal girl's awareness and the man who truly loves his woman needs to respect this deeply from the start of any relationship and most certainly from the beginning of a marriage.

FEELINGS AND THE MIND

So we are made differently in the physical sense but the differences are deeper than they appear. The way men and women think is different. It's not a question of one being superior to the other, it's simply to do with difference. While there seem to be exceptions there usually seems to be more of a 'hot line' between a woman's feelings and her mind than is the case with a man. We speak of a 'woman's intuition'. Somehow she can often feel something to be right or wrong or whatever it might be while a man's more calculating mind takes a bit longer to get there. This difference can be exaggerated, but there is still something true behind it. It can be seen when we have all-female and all-male groups. All-female groups can tend to get petty and 'bitchy' with feelings calling the tune, while all-male gatherings can reveal a callousness, an insensitivity and sometimes a crudeness. Obviously men and women are meant to live in mixed company!

But this ability of a man to stand more easily outside

his feelings and make hard logical decisions means that in marriage he should have the last say if (and only if) the two partners are deadlocked about some important decision. That is one reason why I believe the section in the old prayer book wedding service is right when it asks the bride if she will obey her husband. There has to be an understanding before marriage starts that one of the two holds the casting vote and the man is better equipped for that should it ever have to happen. In my own marriage I doubt whether we have ever been aware of casting votes having to be cast! What we are aware of is that should such a difficult situation arise it will be my job to make the decision.

This obeying the husband business therefore has nothing to do with some tame sort of 'submission'. If I come home drunk and demand my 'husbandly rights' in bed, my wife is under no obligation to give in to such unloving behaviour. A cold bucket of water, well aimed, would be perfectly in order! What it does mean is that no woman should marry a man she doesn't deeply respect.

WORKING WIVES

What about working wives in all this? In these expensive days a high percentage of wives remain at work, especially in the months or years before a family is started and often in later years when the children are older. So we have both partners at work and both coming home tired at the end of the day. When this is the case it is simply not fair or loving for the man to sit down and watch television while his wife switches roles to become cook, washer-up, carpet-sweeper and all the rest of it. *If she has to share the bread-winning then he must share the housekeeping.* I don't think it's the least bit unmanly for men to cook, wash dishes or make beds. Some of us husbands are pretty good cooks – especially when it comes to playing with electric toasters and mixing machines ...

So we are different but we are equals. We seem to be made so that we are better equipped for some things than others. I believe God knew what he was doing when he made human beings. He made men and women so that they needed one another and were meant to share life together.

All healthy society should involve men and women treating each other as equals and yet recognising the weaknesses and strengths that are built into the sexual differences. But a healthy society starts from healthy marriages and if marriages and family life start crumbling then the chances are that society at large may take a fall also.

It really is *that* important.

CHAPTER 4

SEX – GOD'S WEDDING PRESENT

Greetings to all those who have turned to this chapter first! By all means stay with it, but I hope the earlier chapters will also be read before too long.

This chapter is about sexual intercourse which is the way we show our love and longing to be one with each other. It is also the way that this strange and mystical oneness is made and strengthened through the years.

GETTING IT WRONG

Before we can think clearly about sex and about 'making love' we need to get rid of the rubbish that some of us carry around in our minds. It almost seems that more people get it wrong about sex than get it right! Here are three false views which need to be seen as unhelpful.

1. SEX IS 'DIRTY'

Many of us talk as if we are ashamed of our sexuality. We seem to suspect that there is something 'not nice' about this side of life. I have even come across couples who have worried about whether they should pray for forgiveness after intercourse in case there were any lustful feelings during the process.

It seems that some Christians have picked up this false view of things, and the writings of a few ancient monks haven't exactly helped. A moment's thought ought to sort the problem out if one believes in God. Who made men and women as they are? Who is behind the design of the vagina and the penis? Sex is God's idea! He created us male and female.

The Bible never teaches that sex and the enjoyment of our sexuality is wrong. In the creation story we read: 'the man and the woman were both naked, but they were not embarrassed'. In the middle of the Bible is a book called The Song of Songs or The Song of Solomon. It is a love poem written in a quite openly sensual way. In it a man and woman rejoice in the beauty and excitement of each other's bodies.

When St. Paul wanted to find something that would make a good illustration of the togetherness there can be between Christ and his Church, he used the picture of sexual intercourse. It didn't occur to him that this was

33

an unworthy or 'dirty' picture to use.

So we need to see that sexual intercourse is part of God's beautiful and loving plan for the human race. Sadly, over the centuries God's gift of sex has been often made 'dirty' in the way men and women have abused it, but that does not alter the basic truth. Can something that God has planned be anything other than good?

2. SEX IS 'FOR KICKS'

Very often the reaction to something wrong ends up by being just as wrong in a different way.

I think this is what lies behind a great deal of current thinking about sex. The idea of sex being 'dirty' has been rejected. But now, we are told, it is all about success in bed. In the paperback thrillers and the X-certificate movies, sex is all about getting orgasms and the heroes and heroines are nearly always highly skilled 'sexual athletes'. Marriage is less important than pleasure, and who you are in bed with is less important than the feelings he or she can give you.

There are three very serious mistakes being made in all this. The first is in not realising that sexual intercourse is about oneness between two people. Who you are in bed with *does* matter. Intercourse does something to the couple. It makes them one. To go to bed with more than one person is to cheat other people and to cheat oneself.

The second mistake is that this view of sex forgets that the couple are not the only people involved. A stable society depends on stable homes which in turn depend on stable marriages. Desmond Morris in his best-seller *The Naked Ape* suggests that humans are the sexiest animals in the created order. And, writing from a purely zoological angle, he suggests why. Our sexiness, he says, is to keep couples together so that their offspring can be cared for as they grow up.

I agree with him although, as a Christian, I want to stress the deliberate plan of God behind all this. Our sexual versatility is given us not so that we sleep around with several partners, but so as to keep boredom out of a lifelong relationship with one partner.

The third serious mistake with the 'sex for kicks' view is that it can make people feel failures if they don't 'perform' well. Not every act of sexual intercourse ends with a great mutual orgasm. The sex manuals are right in this respect – sexual intercourse has to be learnt. It is something which can be improved with experience.

But even with a couple who are close to each other and have enjoyed a happy sexual relationship for years, there are times when sensations are low. When those times come what matters is not 'success or failure' at something. What matters is that two people who care about each other are expressing their togetherness.

3. SEX IS FOR BABIES

There is a third view that seems to be worthy and right and yet can lead to a great deal of distress. Those who hold this view would agree with all that I have said about sex being part of God's plan. They would probably even agree that it is meant to be enjoyable and fun. However, they would tell us that sexual intercourse is only part of a bigger process, namely the process of having children. In this view, sexual intercourse is only right when having babies is intended. People who hold such a view oppose the idea of family planning.

Of course sexual intercourse is part of the process of having children. But that does not prove that it should not be done unless one wants to have children. By the same way of thinking we could say that because opening the mouth is part of the process of eating we should not open it for anything else!

Such a view is almost always based on belief in a Creator God and the way to answer it is to look again at what the Bible says. As we saw in the first chapter, the creation of man and woman was to build companionship into human existence. Closeness and nakedness is described, but there is no mention of all this being for the sake of having babies.

St. Paul in one of his letters said that avoiding intercourse, except for short periods, was defrauding one's partner. The section in which he said this makes it clear that he was not talking about having more babies. Quite the opposite. His readers were living in dangerous times and he wanted them to have as few family responsibilities as possible.

For most of a woman's cycle she is infertile. If God only wants couples to have sex so as to have babies he hasn't made it easy for us!

No — this view is really a variation of the 'sex is dirty' theme. It can cause great tension in marriages. It can lead to deep emotional illness. It can contribute to break-ups and divorces. St. Paul was right. To get married and then to avoid regular intercourse is to cheat one another.

So – no cheating!

I am not saying that it is right to avoid having children. Far from it. Unless there are medical reasons, I believe it is wrong to plan a childless marriage. All I am saying is that sex is far bigger than a breeding process and to think of it like this is yet another way of cheapening it. We shall be considering family planning in the next chapter.

SIX TRUTHS ABOUT SEX

From all this let me suggest six truths about sexual intercourse:

1. It is a gift from a loving God.
2. It has its boundaries – it is for marriage.
3. It is about love and relationships (even more than feelings).
4. It is meant to be enjoyed.
5. It involves learning and can be improved.
6. It is only partly about having babies.

LOVEMAKING FOR BEGINNERS

There is no shortage of sex manuals and other books about sexual fulfilment. Many of them seem to me to be taking the 'sex for kicks' line but some of them have a much more relationship-centred and Christian view. At the end of this chapter I have listed a few which are well worth reading.

There is a lot to be learnt about lovemaking. Some find this a strange thought. 'Surely if something is "natural" we don't need to learn anything about skills and techniques' – they say. No athlete would agree. God gives us our minds as well as our bodies and we are meant to *think* about the best way to control what is physically natural. That is why a caring couple will have read up about lovemaking or taken skilled advice before the wedding day.

In this section I want to summarise some basic things that newly-weds need to remember.

PRIVACY IS IMPORTANT

If the first attempts at lovemaking are to be as enjoyable as they should be, the couple don't want to have niggling worries that someone could burst in upon them or that they might be overlooked.

RELAXATION IS IMPORTANT

The wedding night can sometimes be a disaster. After a week of excitement and tensions, a late wedding, a full-length reception and a long journey, the couple are likely to arrive at their room exhausted and tense. They need to be realistic. Either the wedding should be set for earlier in the day, or they should spend their first night (in secret) fairly near where the reception took place with further travelling fixed for the next day.

What the couple need is a shower or bath, a meal and some time to calm down. The man may well be eager to begin intercourse but almost certainly the woman needs time to relax.

REALISM IS IMPORTANT

The chances of the first experience of sexual intercourse ending with simultaneous orgasms and being a great technical 'success' are small. That doesn't mean that the experience need be a disappointment. Indeed it may well be one of the most precious memories of one's lifetime. The couple need to approach their first lovemaking with a realistic attitude about this. A sense of humour also helps!

Sexual intercourse is an act which has four phases built into it.

1. FOREPLAY OR AROUSAL

Our bodies are so made that – to put it bluntly – we cannot simply take our clothes off, lie down and have intercourse. We need to be aroused, and this takes longer for the woman than for the man.

A man can be sexually aroused by no more than an erotic thought or the sight of a naked woman. With the woman, however, nothing less than tender wooing and caressing will bring about the emotional and physical condition when she is ready to enjoy the entry of the man's penis.

So our newly-weds in their quiet room will take their time and enjoy the closeness and the sheer loveliness of unhurried kissing, cuddling and gentle words. It is tremendously important for them to realise they are meant to enjoy being sexy. To touch and stroke the intimate parts of each other is not just permissible – it is necessary. There needs to be a considerable amount of helping and advising each other. For example the woman needs to help her husband to learn how to touch and stroke her so that it is most pleasurable.

In particular she needs to help him discover where her clitoris can be found and how best to stimulate it by hand. The clitoris is a tiny organ at the entrance to the vulva area which seems to have been created for no other purpose than sexual pleasure!

Both need to help each other to overcome shyness. A great deal of reassuring is needed (and not only in the early days).

The man is physically ready to enter his wife relatively soon after his penis becomes stiff and erect. It is just possible that tiredness and nervousness will mean that he cannot achieve an erection. He must not worry and she must not make fun of him. Gentle handling and stroking by the woman will almost certainly sort the problem out; and if not, a couple of hours' rest will work wonders!

The woman's body on the other hand takes more time to be ready and needs the patient, gentle stimulation of the partner. A healthy young man may feel impatient here but if he really cares about his wife then he will want her to have the most satisfying experience possible. There is, in fact, a bonus for the man. There is less chance of premature ejaculation upon penetration if the whole tempo of the act is slowed down.

The right time for penetration is when the woman says so. During the foreplay great changes will be taking place in her body. Her heart beat increases (so the songs are right!) her whole body becomes more sensitive, her breathing rate quickens, and she may well become flushed. But the most important point is that in the vaginal area the inner lips will have swollen considerably and the whole area will have become moist and slippery. This moisture is necessary for intercourse to be a pleasurable experience. It may well be that in the early days of marriage a little outside assistance from specially prepared lubricants like KY Jelly make things better still. It makes good sense for a couple to take a tube with them on their honeymoon. It also makes sense to take a soft towel to slip under the woman's hips so that she has no worries about staining the sheets.

During all this time the man must learn restraint and to enjoy *giving* pleasure rather than receiving it (although he will, in fact, receive a great deal). The woman for her part needs to learn that the marriage-bed is one place where she can and must feel free to be totally abandoned. This emotional breakthrough is part of the profound refreshment that intercourse brings.

2. PENETRATION AND INCREASING EXCITEMENT

When the woman feels aroused and senses that her sex organs are ready she should signal her husband to come in to her.

In the case of a virgin we have to consider the fact of the hymen or maidenhead. This is a membrane that is stretched across the back part of the outside opening of the vagina. The intact hymen is the traditional evidence of a woman's virginity, however, the truth is that a hymen can be practically absent from birth or can be broken or stretched through modern sanitary tampons or through some types of activity or accident.

Doctors or Family Planning Clinics are usually prepared to stretch or break this membrane before marriage and there is no moral reason and every practical reason for this to be done. If the hymen is left intact for the wedding night then doctor's advice should be taken as to the best way for the initial stretching to be carried out. It is far better, however, to have it dealt with by the doctor. Virginity is precious but it has absolutely nothing to do with the state of the hymen and old wives' tales can be forgotten.

But even if the bride has been sensible enough to check that her hymen will cause no problems, the first act of penetration needs to be gentle and careful. The position of the couple has a great effect upon this. There are an amazing number of positions and variations possible for intercourse and variety is the spice of life in this as in most matters. However, it is probably sensible in first intercourse for the woman to relax on her back with her legs apart and slightly flexed or even with her feet flat on the bed and her knees drawn up. As her husband moves his body onto her he should take most of the weight upon his elbows. Twelve stones of ardent manhood can

41

be asking too much of any young bride and doesn't exactly add to her enjoyment of the exercise!

It is probably best for the woman herself to guide the penis into the vagina and the entry needs to be slow and gentle. It can be uncomfortable for her and there is a real chance of premature ejaculation for him. If the husband has spread some KY Jelly on his penis it may well add to the woman's comfort. After entry has taken place immediate thrusting should be avoided. A new chapter in the couple's relationship has begun and it makes a great deal of sense for them to lie quietly in each other's arms and take in the sheer wonder of it.

When the over-excitement and tension of penetration has passed and before there is any chance of either partner's arousal beginning to fade, gentle movement needs to begin. The fact that the husband's penis is in the vagina does not mean that there is not room for his hand to move down to the area of the clitoris to help give added stimulation. The two, now sexually united, need to keep each other informed as to 'where they are'. He needs to try to hold back his climax to allow her slower arousal pattern to catch up. The ideal is for both to have their orgasm at the same time but this needs skill and is highly unlikely to happen at first.

3. ORGASM OR CLIMAX

Orgasm for the man is the climax of the sex act when in a deeply pleasurable way all the build-up of excitement and tension seems to explode and a tremendous sense of release comes over the whole body. The explosion flings out the milky mixture of seminal fluid with a re-markable force through the urethra tube in the penis.

Once the man has 'come' in this way his feelings and his erection subside remarkably quickly. This is where he differs from his wife. Her arousal takes longer and she also takes longer to subside. Her orgasm has a different quality about it also. It is not such a sudden explosion. At climax she enters a period of high pleasurable sensation with more than one peak to it.

A caring husband will remember this and after his own orgasm keep thrusting in his wife as long as it is physically possible before his erection dispels. When he can no longer help her in this way she may well find that continued massaging of the area around the clitoris will add to her enjoyment and sense of release. Again quiet, unabashed conversation is the secret.

What the man must never do after his climax is to detach himself and roll over satisfied with no thought to the woman's continuing emotional and physical needs.

4. THE AFTERGLOW

After climax a deep sense of joyous relaxation usually comes over both partners. After a period of great excitement and tension all seems to be a glowing peacefulness. This is a time for tired and happy words and caresses. It very often ends by both falling into the loveliest sort of sleep a person can experience.

WEDDING NIGHT FAILURES?

There is no such thing as a failure on one's wedding night if the couple have done their best to show and share their love for each other. There are, however, one or two set-backs which can affect the first attempts at intercourse.

Perhaps the two most common set-backs are overtiredness and tension on the part of the bride which stops her body preparing itself for intercourse. Should this be seen to be the case after twenty minutes of foreplay then the truly loving husband should suggest that they simply go to sleep in each other's arms. A few hours sleep is likely to put things right.

However, the truly loving woman may well feel that her ardent husband needs some emotional and sexual release and she may feel that she could bring this about by manual stimulation of his penis or by moving her body against him until she senses that she has brought this about. Set down in cold print this can appear almost distasteful and crude. In the setting of a loving and caring relationship it is far from being so.

Another common 'failure' in early intercourse is premature ejaculation. The man, upon entry or even before, can hold back no longer and climaxes. As soon as this happens his erection begins to subside.

The last thing he should suspect is that he is going to have a 'problem' with this. It is very understandable in the circumstances. The wife should reassure him. If she feels the need for more stimulation at the time then she can ask for his help and this will make him feel better.

And, once again, some sleep or even dozing may restore his energies for a further adventure!

When you have just got married and face a whole lifetime of sleeping together, any early set-backs are of little importance. And no set-back need blot out the sheer joy of being totally together at last!

FIVE REMINDERS FOR THE HONEYMOON

1. Have you sorted out the family planning side and received whatever requisites that you will need?
2. Has the woman's hymen been checked?

3. Have both of you read something basic about love-making or taken advice?
4. Have you talked together frankly about intercourse?
5. Have you packed some KY Jelly and a soft towel?

For Further Reading:
The Book of Love, Dr. David Delvin, New English Library
Intended for Pleasure, Ed and Gaye Wheat, Scripture Union
The Act of Marriage, Tim and Beverly La Haye, Zondervan (U.S.A.)

CHAPTER 5

PLANNING A FAMILY

There are, of course, other words for family planning such as contraception or birth control. I prefer the term I have used because it is positive. It does not talk about avoiding having children but about having a family at the right time. I believe this is a very important way to use the intelligence that our Creator has given us.

STRONG OBJECTIONS

Some religious people have strong objections to family planning and that really means that they are saying that intercourse is only meant by God for the purpose of having children. I have already tried to show that this is not a proper way to understand what is written in the Bible.

There are, however, other very sincere people who would disagree with me at this point and say that they *do* believe in intercourse without the intention to conceive but there are natural ways of doing this. What they point to is that there is a 'safe period' during the woman's cycle when she cannot conceive. Intercourse can take place during that time and all will be well.

There are several points to make here. First we should note that those who argue like this are stating positively that intercourse is good in itself and not only when having children is intended. Three cheers for that!

Second, while they have given us the freedom to enjoy intercourse for its own sake, they have not given us a way of doing it that is free from anxiety. The whole safe-period is far from fool-proof. There are some doctors who reject it out of hand as a genuine method of family planning.

Third, seeing that we are 'allowed' to plan our families and to enhance our lives by intercourse as a form of physical communion without intending to have children, I fail to see why we cannot make use of some method that, as much as possible, takes away anxiety about conceiving. At this point some who hold the view I am criticising say there is an important difference between 'natural' contraception and artificial contraception. God has built in a natural family planning system they say, but sinful man has thought up artificial ways of doing it.

Quite honestly this sort of view is emotional rather than intelligent. God has given us intelligence and reason. He has put us in a world where there is food to eat and where there are chemicals to be extracted which have properties we can discover and put to use. I call this 'natural'. I can see no difference in the end between family planning by the 'safe period' (with charts and thermometers at the ready) and family planning by the 'pill' or by such methods as the sheath or cap. The only difference is that these other methods are more effective.

So I hope my readers will think sensibly about family planning, and do this thinking *well before the wedding day*. In fact I would argue that this is something that calls for agreement before even getting engaged. This is an area that calls for expert advice, and organisations such as the Family Planning Association have been set up to make sure that the best advice is available. Very many family doctors prefer to guide their patients on this personally and like to be asked. With regard to such methods as the contraceptive pill it is important for the woman's medical history to be known and no-one is better placed to judge this than one's own regular doctor.

Some clinics, however, offer the opportunity for the couple to come together to talk things over and this is all to the good. Decisions in this area of life should be joint decisions.

If anyone feels very deeply on grounds of conscience that the 'safe period' is the only approach to family planning that they will accept, then they should talk it over very carefully with a sympathetic doctor. It will probably mean that they will have to understand how to work charts and temperature-taking. Probably the best advice can be had from the Catholic Marriage Advisory Service who have given this matter a great deal of thought and are willing to advise non-Catholic couples.

Unless a couple are agreed before marriage about this approach and unless they take skilled advice, then the chances of an unwanted pregnancy early in marriage are very high. This is a before-the-wedding top priority.

METHODS AVAILABLE

It may be of help, before talking to the experts, to be aware of the main approaches to family planning that are in use. The order in which they are listed is not to be taken as an order of preferences!

1. ORAL CONTRACEPTIVES (THE PILL). This is taken by the woman. It needs to be prescribed by a doctor.

Advantages
(a) It is extremely effective.
(b) It can be used to delay a period which can be valuable in such matters as timing the wedding and honeymoon.
(c) There is no preparation (such as fitting a cap or condom) necessary before lovemaking.
(d) The woman is protected against unwanted pregnancy at all times.

Disadvantages
(a) Some women cannot have the pill prescribed for medical reasons.
(b) Few doctors like women over thirty-five to use it.
(c) There can sometimes be unpleasant side effects – nausea, weight gain (and loss), bleeding between periods, amongst others.
(d) The woman has to remember to take her pill every day.

2. INTRA-UTERINE DEVICE (I.U.D.). This is a flexible plastic loop which is inserted by the doctor into the woman's uterine cavity. How it works is not fully understood.

Advantages
(a) It is very effective.
(b) As with the pill no preparation is necessary before intercourse.
(c) There is no regime of pill-taking for the woman to remember.
(d) The I.U.D. can be left in place for several years without apparent harm.

Disadvantages
(a) The I.U.D. has to be inserted by a doctor and has to be removed by a doctor when a pregnancy is desired.
(b) The I.U.D. can be expelled and the woman has to learn a weekly check-routine.
(c) There can be some discomfort in the first few days after insertion.
(d) It is possible that the I.U.D. works by aborting rather than preventing conception. This is not certain, but some feel that if aborting is the working principle of the I.U.D. it is a morally unacceptable method.

3. THE DIAPHRAGM OR CAP. This is a fine rubber cap which the woman learns to insert in the vagina before intercourse takes place. It must be used in conjunction with a contraceptive jelly or cream. Expert advice and measurement is needed from a doctor or nurse.

Advantages

(a) It is very effective if used correctly.
(b) Neither partner need be aware of its presence when fitted correctly.
(c) The cap can be left in place for over a day if necessary.
(d) There are no side effects.

Disadvantages

(a) Intercourse should only take place during the time that the jelly is effective. Further jelly must be added if intercourse is desired after that time.
(b) The cap needs to be carefully maintained and needs to be regularly inspected for wear and tear.
(c) The woman's internal measurements can change (especially after pregnancy) so annual checks are advisable.
(d) The woman has to prepare herself before intercourse and for some this can be a 'turn-off'.

4. **THE SHEATH OR CONDOM.** This is worn over the penis by the man.

Advantages

(a) If used correctly it is fairly effective. It is extremely effective if the wife uses a vaginal contraceptive jelly at the same time.
(b) There are no side effects.
(c) Condoms can be bought 'over the counter' and so are freely available.
(d) They can assist some men with the problem of premature ejaculation.

Disadvantages

(a) They have to be applied to the erect penis during

the foreplay phase and this is a 'turn-off' for some.
(b) They have to be disposed of after use.
(c) Care needs to be taken upon withdrawal to avoid a condom coming off.
(d) They reduce sensation for the man and may require added lubrication to avoid discomfort to the woman.

5. CREAMS, FOAMS AND JELLIES. These have to be applied internally by the woman immediately before intercourse.

Advantages
(a) They are available without prescription.
(b) No fittings are necessary and there is nothing to remember outside of actual sexual activity.

Disadvantages
(a) A less effective method than those listed above.
(b) There is the need for application (usually with a special applicator) immediately before intercourse.
(c) There is a greater amount of discharge following intercourse.

6. THE SAFE PERIOD. This involves restricting intercourse to the times when the wife is likely to be infertile.

Advantages
(a) No regime of pills and no off-putting application of chemicals, caps or condoms.
(b) No side effects.
(c) Next to no expense!

Disadvantages
(a) Not a very effective method in practice.
(b) There is a need to master the facts of how the woman's cycle works. Using charts and temperature taking are all part of the method.
(c) Approximately one in six women menstruate too irregularly to use this method.

7. COITUS INTERRUPTUS (WITHDRAWAL). This involves the man withdrawing immediately before ejaculation.

Advantages – none!

Disadvantages
(a) Not effective.
(b) Sperms are released before ejaculation.
(c) The full experience of the sex act is ruined.
(d) Can cause emotional harm.

8. STERILISATION. This means a small operation for the man (vasectomy) or a larger operation in the case of the woman (tubal ligation). Some men fear that this operation could affect their sex drive, but there is no evidence that this is so.

Advantages
(a) Totally effective as a means of avoiding conception. (There is a short time after a vasectomy operation when conception can still occur.)
(b) After the operation there are no regimes of pills to remember or things to do before intercourse.
(c) Vasectomy is a very slight operation with little discomfort.

Disadvantages
- (a) These are virtually irreversable operations, and in the case of tubal ligation the operation is a major one with a slight degree of risk.
- (b) Such a drastic approach only makes sense after a number of children have been born.

THE REAL PURPOSE

The true purpose of family planning is the planning of a family! Every child has the right to feel that he or she was *wanted* and is cherished. Methods of contraception give us the chance to have richer sexual relationships and these ought to make us parents with a deeper love for each other. Every child needs a home where the parents are in love with each other.

But all this is assuming that the children are conceived and born! It has to be admitted that family planning methods can make us more self-centred and greedy. Children are delayed and delayed while more and more material possessions are amassed. Sometimes when they are born they sense a resentment for taking away parental freedom or because they create untidiness in the show-room house their parents have taken years to put together.

Make sure this never happens with you!

CHAPTER 6

SETTING UP HOME

One of the fascinating facts of life is that while many houses and flats are identical, no two *homes* are alike. The homes that we make for ourselves have their own character – or perhaps we should say, they show something about the character of the people who set them up.

That is one reason why it's a good thing to visit the home of the person you are courting! We make homes and homes make us, to some extent, in return.

WHAT IS A HOME?

What is a home? That is not an easy question. I would suggest that a home is made up of the following parts:

1. *A building*. This is the least important part of a *home,* but of course you can't have a home without it!
2. *Furnishings*. This is the next to least important element in a home but the furnishings reveal a great deal. They show how much we value possessions.
3. *The way the house is kept*. Is it kept in such a way that you feel the *things* are more important than the people? Is it kept in such a way that you feel order and tidiness matter and pleasantness of colour or shape is important? Is it a place for people to be human in or it is a place where people keep themselves firmly under control to avoid disturbing the tidiness? Is it a place for people to come to or simply a base of operations from which people go?
4. *The people*. This is the most important part of any home. A home is basically the place where the people can be at their most 'real'. Many young couples make mistakes here. They fit out their home before they have discovered what a home is about and what they themselves as a couple are all about. They can have a tussle between the furnishings and themselves and sometimes they lose the battle!

What I am really saying in all this is that setting up a home is far more than collecting things for the 'bottom drawer'. It is all about making up your mind about your sense of values. Do people matter more than things? Do you want to have a house that is the envy of all the neighbours? Do you want to create a place where people can come and feel relaxed?

Obviously I am biased here. As a Christian I think we are meant to create *people-centred* homes rather than *thing-centred* homes. That does *not* mean that there is not a proper place for beautiful things. Colour is part of God's glorious creation. Some colours go better together than others. Shape and proportion make all the difference between beauty and ugliness. And, of course, comfortable chairs and comfortable beds are extremely important. All my talk about a home helping humans to be more real is a bit ridiculous if all the chairs in a room force one's backbone into a figure 'S'!

BEWARE OF MATERIALISM

But Jesus warned against materialism. He pointed out that there were more valuable things than money and possessions. He said:

Do not store up riches for yourselves here on earth, where moths and rust destroy, and robbers break in and steal. Instead, store up riches for yourself in heaven ... For your heart will always be where your riches are ... You cannot serve both God and money.

(Matthew 6: 19–24)

Tucked away in those words are some very important lessons for us all. Let's look at them.

1. *Riches and possessions can come and go.* It may not be moths or rust or robbers that snatch away our prized possessions or savings. It could be a firm going bankrupt, or mounting inflation or a string of unexpected repair

bills to house and car. In any case, as the old saying goes, you can't take it with you when you die. Of course we need money to live on (quite a bit of it!) and we need somewhere to live, chairs to sit on and all the rest. God knows that. What Jesus warned against is 'storing up' riches – living as if money and possessions were the most important things in the world. To go that way in life is to head for disappointments and – at the end of the road – nothing short of despair.

2. *Money and possessions can rule our lives.* Jesus said that our hearts and affections will always be controlled by whatever we think is most valuable. If what we want most is a gadget-filled kitchen, or a brand-new car or any other *thing*, then we will be less interested in the welfare of people, including the people we are married to. Materialism has wrecked many a marriage.

What Jesus was talking about, of course, was putting God first. When we do that then we will value other people as well because we will see that God loves them as much as he loves us. And when that happens, possessions find their proper place. It is not that money and possessions are unimportant. Far from it. The secret is not to let them become more important than they should be.

3. *Money and possessions can become idols.* 'You cannot serve both God and money,' Jesus said. Obviously he believed that we can end up serving money (and what it can buy) in the way we should be serving God, so we can't say we haven't been warned!

A WHOLE HOST OF THINGS

So much for the serious side to setting up a home. But

what about the sheer fun of it! We do need to get together a whole host of things and it is a chance to gather things we like and that express our taste and outlook on life. It may be that we do not need too much for the first year or so if we are going to live in furnished accommodation; but sooner or later we shall have to set up our own place.

Let us imagine that you are establishing yourselves in a small flat or set of rooms which consist of:

1 Bedroom
1 Lounge/dining room
1 Bathroom, W.C.
1 Kitchen

Let us assume that you have to furnish and equip all this and that you don't want to spend more than you have to. Here are some ideas.

1. *The bedroom.*
First of all I strongly advise getting a good quality, new bed. A good bed should last up to fifteen years (perhaps longer if you replace the mattress). A poor quality bed can let you down (literally) in half the time. Alas, good beds cost money. If you have parents or friends willing to store some furniture then it's worth shopping during the Sales for the bed. I would not recommend anything narrower than four foot six.

If you like a firm or fairly hard bed then money can be saved by making a Swedish-style timber base and buying a mattress only. My wife and I got a design sheet from our local timber merchant for one of these, and the same firm supplied us with the timber cut to size plus all the fittings. Mind you – one needs to have some joinery skill (and fortunately my wife has!).

59

Blankets and sheets are becoming increasingly expensive and it is well worth considering a continental quilt or 'duvet'. It is wise to avoid the cheaper quilt-fillings, going instead for the best quality terylene, or better still, down or feather fillings. (Asthma sufferers might have to avoid these, however.) It is best to go for the biggest possible size (usually called king size) as some quilts are cut too neatly for a four-foot-six bed.

With regard to items like dressing-tables, wardrobes and chests-of-drawers it pays to look out for second-hand items. These are often advertised in local newspapers and in shop windows. Sometimes one can find a second-hand furniture shop nearby. Then of course there is the good old jumble sale. What you have to look for is something made of real wood rather than some sort of veneer or blockboard and melamine. Once you find one, it can be rubbed down and re-stained and/or polished using some of the new polyurethane finishes.

Of course there are several firms marketing easy-to-assemble furniture at very reasonable prices. These are well worth considering, although very often second-hand furniture will prove to be more solid and a better buy.

Floor covering is another expense. If the floors consist of wooden boards (as opposed to blockboard) then these can be turned into something very attractive. A sander can expose a fresh natural wood surface and this again can be coated with an attractive polyurethane finish which can be bought from the local DIY store. The end result can be a delightful polished wood floor on which you can put rugs. When we did this in our house, we were able to hire an industrial sander from the local hire-out centre. This made short work of the floor space – and nearly made short work of a few toes! Your Yellow Pages should help you find a local hiring firm.

Carpeting, if preferred, does not have to be top quality

in bedrooms as they take surprisingly little wear over the years. Look out for bargains in flood stock sales, and second-hand carpets advertised in the local press. Again carpet warehouses often sell off ends of rolls of broadloom carpeting at bargain prices. If your bedroom is not too oddly shaped you can fit foam-backed carpeting fairly easily yourself.

Curtains don't have to be lined and again one can find second-hand bargains. Friends or relatives have often a set of curtains which they don't need and which can be adapted. Chain stores like Woolworth's stock modestly priced ready-made curtains, some of which are very presentable and of pleasing design.

2. *The lounge/dining room.*

We have already discussed floor coverings and curtains. The only real difference with this sort of room is that the floor will take very much more wear. Any carpeting you buy ought ideally to be of better quality and it is best to avoid patterns. A good carpet will last a fair number of years and may have to match several sets of other furnishings. Plain, 'neutral' colours are probably the best to go for.

To eat requires that you have a table and chairs. It may be that you have been fortunate enough to have received a dining-room suite as a wedding present. It is probably wisest to start with a fold-down or extending table. Even in the early days of marriage there will be times when you want to sit six or so down for a meal. That again suggests looking for half-a-dozen dining-table chairs. If you are buying new I would suggest you go for a very cheap, melamine-topped table and expect to relegate it to other uses later on, or go for a good quality suite that will last you all your life. Anything in between might be a disappointment.

Here again it pays to look at the small-ads in the local papers, to visit second-hand furniture shops and jumble sales!

What goes on the dining table needs to be stored somewhere – crockery, cutlery, glasses, table linen or mats and all the rest. One approach to this problem is to keep most of it in the kitchen. Another is to have a sideboard in the dining area. They are immensely useful things and have extra value in providing a surface area near the table where things can be put when you are having an extra special meal.

I strongly recommend equipping yourself with a basic, matching set of crockery which is widely sold. Every generation seems to have at least two or three styles of crockery that are in the shops for several years. It ensures that replacements are easy to find when things get broken – and things *do* get broken. My wife always claims that crockery 'jumps out at her' but I am sceptical! These things just happen and if you can't easily get matched replacements you very soon have a shoddy-looking table setting.

When it comes to cutlery there are several patterns of reasonably priced stainless steel knives, forks and spoons available these days. Often one gets a canteen of cutlery as a wedding present but there is some sense in having a presentable second-string set for everyday, knockabout use.

We have been assuming a lounge/diner so this requires compactness in the various items we put together. It also assumes that we need to give thought to the 'sitting room' aspect. One obvious thing to go for is a three-piece suite, but here I would advise some caution. It might well be better to go for a couple of easy chairs and a 'put-you-up' so that you can have guests staying overnight. Keep a look-out for second-hand put-you-ups. They are extremely useful items of furniture. And always check that they are comfortable to sleep on before you buy. Another approach to this is to go for a divan without a headboard which you can cover, push against the wall, and equip with cushions so that people can use it as a settee.

Economically-minded people might want to think of the ease of re-covering, when they think about buying easy chairs. For example, a good 'cottage'-style wooden chair with loose cushions can be made to last for two or three lifetimes. As long as the woodwork is sound, one simply recovers or replaces the cushions. Old easy chairs (and fireside patterns) can often be given a new lease of life through fitting stretch covers. There are some very good patterns and fabrics available from the various makers. Actual, full-scale re-upholstery can prove very expensive and unless one is well advised it is not wise to buy second-hand and then re-upholster. It could turn out to be a very expensive approach to saving money!

A big floor-cushion can be fun and is something that can be made at home. Some sort of coffee-table is also a good idea and a do-it-yourself approach here could save a great deal of money. Other things to bear in mind are the need for something on which to put things like a radio or record-player or small television set. Again a table lamp or taller lamp stand can give the room character through off-centre lighting. Lighting makes a huge difference. We have found that a coal-effect electric fire can also give a focal point to the lounge area of the sort of room we are discussing.

3. *The kitchen.*
The most important item of equipment is the cooker. If you have to buy one, it is wise to check whether gas is available before you decide to buy a gas cooker. It may sound crazy but it could save you from making a very ex-

pensive mistake! It is basically wise not to buy (new or second-hand) before you know the shape and size of the kitchen. Once again the small ads can lead to bargains but, in the case of gas cookers, it is important to check that the cooker being sold is compatible with the gas which is available in the area.

Refrigerators and washing machines are also often advertised in the local press and in small shop window displays. As a general rule I have found that the 'posher' the area, the cheaper the second-hand price. So it's worth looking around.

A 'Burco' boiler is another approach to washing but in the early days of marriage the local launderette is as good a solution to the washing problem as any.

If the kitchen is big enough to eat in it will need a melamine-topped surface area or table which can be used for meals and also for the preparation of food. In this sort of situation it is best to keep cutlery and crockery in the kitchen. Stools take up less space than chairs with backs and a high kitchen stool is a very valuable friend to those with tired legs.

The window-covering can be a roller-blind, and some very attractive and reasonably priced do-it-yourself kits are now available. The floor covering needs to be able to cope with damp and this rules out carpets. Lino tiles or linoleum itself would seem to be the best things to go for.

Other items which you will need:
Iron and ironing board
Set of saucepans, frying pan (get a good one)
Casserole dish
Electric or whistling kettle
Teapot
Cutlery (or in living room)

Half a dozen of: cups, saucers, tea plates, dinner plates, cereal/soup/pudding bowls, tumblers, mugs (or keep in living room)

Washing-up bowl and drainer

Kitchen utensils e.g. mixing bowls, whisk (electric or hand-operated) can-opener (very important for expert cooks!), breadboard and knife, measuring jug, wooden spoon, rolling-pin, pastry-board, kitchen knives, peeler

Bread bin, storage jars

Kitchen scales

Tea towels, dishcloths, apron (husband-sized)

Pedal bin (plus plastic liners)

4. *The bathroom and toilet.*

I am presuming that you do not have to buy a bath! It is worth checking, however, what the bath is made from. If it is fibre-glass in construction make sure that abrasive cleaners are never used.

Once again the floor surface needs to be one that can cope with splashes of water. Linoleum or tiles is the best answer. Those who like a luxury touch however can buy nylon rubber-backed carpets and they cope with the damp fairly well.

As with the kitchen a roller-blind is ideal as the window-covering. It is worth checking what sort of glass is fitted in the window! You may need to fit something like net curtains if the window is plain glass. It can be rather embarrassing to get into your first bath in your new home and find the neighbours taking an interest!

Other things to bear in mind include:

Towels

Bath mat

Face cloths, nail brush

Hooks for face cloths
Bathroom cabinet (or sufficient shelf space)
Towel rail
Toilet-roll holder
Lavatory brush

All this is merely a basic look at what you might need to set up home. As you await the wedding it makes sense to draw up a list of the presents that would most help you set up home. This can then be passed around friends and relatives to help them in thinking about suitable presents. Such a move avoids the embarrassment of duplication. (There are not many shops that will swap three ironing boards for a duvet!)

There is a great deal of sense in sticking to the very basic essentials at first and then building up the home over the early years, developing the style and mood that is 'you'.

Your local library and any good bookshop will have books available that go into greater detail on all these matters. Such books are well worth buying and can, indirectly, be a great help in the task of working out the sort of home you want to set up.

Chapter 7

PLANNING THE WEDDING

The day before my own wedding I nearly called the whole thing off! My future mother-in-law said something to me and it was the last straw. I just got up, stormed out of the house and went home to my own mother.

By the time I had finished telling her all about it it was obvious what I had to do. I turned round, walked the mile back to my future mother-in-law and apologised. The whole thing was ridiculous. Meanwhile Mary, my wife-to-be, was so distracted with all the fuss that she quite forgot that she had toothache and was due at the dentist!

I have often noticed other young couples getting keyed-up in the last few days before the wedding. What I had to realise was that it wasn't my wedding! It was a family occasion belonging to the bride's family. I am not joking – that really is what the wedding day is all about. Whenever I am interviewing couples who have asked me to take the ceremony, I always try to explain that the wedding is a family occasion even more than a personal one for the young couple. And so it should be. We don't value families enough.

And don't forget – it's usually the bride's parents who are footing the bill for everything!

WEDDING ETIQUETTE

We don't get married every day and there are a great many things to remember. That's why it makes a great deal of sense to go along to your local bookseller and buy a book on 'wedding etiquette'. They always tend to be a little quaint – but they are mines of information and very helpful.

I will not try to give a full guide to all that you have to do. The books I mentioned do that. My purpose here is to set out some of the basic things the young couple need to remember.

1. FIX THE DATE AND PLACE

It is usually best to fix a date several months in advance. It takes time for banns to be read if you are planning a church wedding and it is often difficult to get a place for a wedding reception unless you book early.

Let me be quite personal for a moment. Before you

announce the date the girl needs to do a few sums about her monthly cycle. It is not ideal to go off on your honeymoon and begin a period the following day. If the girl is going to use the contraceptive pill there are ways of taking this to delay a period and her doctor or family planning clinic can explain how this can be done.

Obviously one of the first people to be approached should be the minister at the church. May I make a plea for my hard-worked fellow clergymen. Contrary to popular opinion they do not only work for one day a week. Many of the clergy I know do not take a regular day off. They usually suffer from continuous calls on the phone and at the door. That is why many of them set aside particular times in the week when they can deal with enquiries about baptisms and weddings. Please check on this sort of thing before you arrive on his doorstep at what might be a bad time.

He may well have other couples booked in for weddings on the day you want which is another reason why it is best to decide on a date several months ahead. A bit of juggling with the time may have to be done.

It is important to realise that a church wedding is a Christian service of worship. It combines the legal registration of the marriage with prayers and praise to the heavenly Father who brought you together. Because this is so I believe there needs to be some sincere belief on the part of the couple. If this is not so then the whole thing is play-acting and you start your married life with an act of hypocrisy. I've heard of some people who only asked for a church wedding so that they could have all the trimmings and a nice background for the photographs.

But what about if you only half-believe? You are not too sure. You do not pretend to know all the answers. You wish you could have the sort of faith that others have, but somehow it has not yet happened for you? If that is how you feel I would urge you to start your married life in church. Talk it over together and make up your minds to start your married life determined to find out more about Christ and to take sides with all that he stands for. Tell this to the minister you visit – it will probably make his day!

If you are Anglicans the wedding would normally be in the parish church of one of the couple – traditionally the bride's parish church. If you live in two different parishes the Banns of Marriage will have to be read in both those churches. It may be that one or other of you has become a member of a third parish church, and that is where you want to be married. In such a case you will need to be on the electoral roll of this third parish church. This is very simply organised – indeed if you are a member you will probably already have arranged this so that you can vote at the annual church meeting. In this situation (and it happened to me) you will have to arrange for the Banns to be read in *all three churches*.

Yes – and it means three lots of fees!

The reading of the Banns of Marriage takes place in the public services of the church for three successive Sundays and couples should be in attendance at those particular services. The object of the exercise is to give the community in which you live a chance to stop the wedding taking place if they can show evidence that the law would be broken. The only evidence that could do this would be to show that the couple are related within what is known as the 'prohibited degrees' (see Appendix D), that one or the other is legally married to someone else; or if one or other of the parties to the marriage is under age (eighteen) and does not have written consent from parents.

If a wedding has to be arranged at short notice then

the minister can advise about obtaining a common licence but this is much more expensive than the cost of reading the Banns.

Free Church and Roman Catholic wedding arrangements differ slightly but basically the key is to give plenty of notice and to find out when to see the minister or priest. Problems only emerge when people want to rush things. But even then, if a wedding has to be in a hurry for some reason, *go and ask*!

CIVIL WEDDINGS

If you plan to have a civil wedding then application needs to be made to the Superintendent Registrar of Marriages in the districts where the couple live and where they intend to marry. A form will have to be filled out and, normally, twenty-one days would have to elapse before the certificate can be issued making the way clear for the marriage to be conducted.

Once again, if time is short, more expensive arrangements can be made for a marriage by Certificate and Licence. Only one of the couple needs to make the application (the correct term is 'giving notice') but at least one of the two must have been living in the Registrar's district for at least fifteen days before the giving of notice.

DIVORCED PEOPLE

The churches and their clergy are completely at 'sixes and sevens' over remarriage of divorced people. And for the best of reasons. On the one hand we Christians believe that marriage is special. We can never help along a sort of change-your-partners approach to marriage.

Marriage is a picture of God's faithful, unbreakable

link with those who trust him. The wedding vows are all about 'till death us do part'. We must not do anything to undermine marriage.

On the other hand – people matter and God loves all of us equally. We make mistakes in all areas of life and marriage is no exception. So when a divorced person asks for remarriage in church we clergy find ourselves being torn apart.

Many Free Churches will remarry divorced persons. Roman Catholics have a different approach altogether which is difficult to explain but the gist of it is that while they will not remarry divorced persons, there are certain sorts of first marriages that they do not recognise as true marriages. In such cases they will consider what others would call a second marriage.

Anglicans officially do not remarry divorced persons. In fact some Anglicans will. Those who feel in all conscience that they cannot do so, would be anxious to arrange a church ceremony to follow the civil ceremony in which the new marriage can be commended to God in prayer.

Ask about it and do not interpret any refusal to take a church wedding as a personal rejection. It probably hurts the parson as much as anyone else.

WHITE WEDDING?

Sometimes a couple who have already slept together, or who have 'slept around' in the past, wonder whether they ought to marry in church or whether the bride ought to be in white.

As far as I am concerned the key to all this is your sincerity for the future and not whether there are skeletons in the cupboard regarding the past. Sexual sins are no different from any other sins. If we are sorry about them then they can be forgiven. The forgiveness of God is total. I love the one of the many phrases in the Bible about God's forgiveness:

I have swept your sins away like a cloud
Come back to me; I am the one who saves you.
Isaiah 44:22

God is the God of new starts so why not see your wedding as a new start – just the two of you plus a heavenly Father watching over you for all the days ahead.

And a white wedding? Why not? To quote the book of Isaiah again:

You are stained red with sin, but I will wash you as clean as snow. Isaiah 1:18

White seems to be the ideal colour for the forgiven sinner, and that is the most that we ever can be from God's point of view. The exciting thing is that we can be forgiven.

2. THE RECEPTION

This is, officially, a matter for the bride's parents to deal with. Books on wedding etiquette are very helpful in setting out all the things to bear in mind. One option is not to have a reception at all!

However, it is one of those occasions when you can have a large number of family and friends together and such times are surprisingly rare.

The bride's parents, then, are in charge of the arrangements – it is *their* party! If they are wise they will want to talk the matter over carefully with the couple. If this happens it is thoughtful to remember that receptions can be *very* expensive. A sit-down meal for seventy people or so runs into hundreds of pounds.

There are four choices:

1. A reception in a hotel or restaurant with a sit-down meal.
2. A reception at a hotel or restaurant with a buffet meal (cheaper).
3. A reception in a hired hall or at home with outside caterers (cheaper still).
4. A reception at the bride's home with self-catering (cheapest of all and absolutely 'proper' according to the etiquette books!).

Whatever you plan to do, it is best to book early.

3. PHOTOGRAPHS

Photographers cost a considerable amount these days. They have to make a living and they work with expensive equipment and materials. A very elaborate colour album can cost over £100 in some places.

If you plan to save here and use amateur photographers it is not always ideal. You could be straining a friendship if your amateur photographer friend makes a hash of it! (However some of us amateur photographers are pretty good!)

4. OTHER THINGS TO BEAR IN MIND

It is wise for the bride's parents and for the couple to draw up a check-list of things that need to be remembered. Here are some of them:

Florist

Cars

Bride's dress (buy, hire or make?)

Bridesmaids' dresses (buy, hire or make?)

Bridegroom's suit (buy or hire or one you already have?)

Best man's suit (if hiring)

Ring or rings

Wedding stationery (don't leave printing to the last moment)

Presents for best man and bridesmaids

Male friends to act as ushers at the church

It's worth remembering when you look through a list like this that all of it is about man-made traditions. There's no law that says you have to do or have any or all of these traditional things apart from the wedding ring. You can simply put up the banns or give notice, go with a couple of witnesses and get married. Just like that. And I must say – it certainly sounds cheaper!

5. THE HONEYMOON

Yet again here is a good reason for planning a wedding early. Holidays often take some booking-up.

There is no reason why one *has* to have a honeymoon. Certainly I think that it is foolish to spend a great deal of money going to some exotic resort when there is so much cash needed for setting up a home. Some couples prefer to go straight to their new home and start their married life there. It gives them time to settle in before one or both has to go back to work.

However, I am glad that my new wife and I managed to get away on our own for a few days (on a boat). Getting away allows the two of you to relax and to enjoy your togetherness without people you know calling on you (or even worse – obviously trying to keep out of your way!). Often the last week or so before the wedding has been so hectic that the newly-weds are in a state of emotional exhaustion by the evening of the wedding day. Time is obviously needed to unwind and that is what a honeymoon is meant for.

So if you can get away for a honeymoon – do!

For Further Reading:
Getting Married in Church, Mary Batchelor, Lion Publishing
Wedding Etiquette – properly explained Vernon Heaton, Elliot Paperfront Books

CHAPTER 8

AVOIDING THE PITFALLS

I was travelling home on a train full of London commuters a good many years ago, and couldn't help hearing a couple of girls talking to each other. They were talking about boys and comparing notes on some that they knew. Something that one of them said has stuck in my memory ever since:

'Oh, I could never marry him! He doesn't believe in divorce!'

I thought about those words all the rest of the way home. I have certainly thought about them over the years. What was she saying about marriage? Did she believe that you can only go into marriage after you have carefully built in an escape route? Was she saying that commitment 'till death us do part' is a thing of the past?

One thing is certainly clear to me. There have been a great many unhappy marriages over the years and divorce is a growing factor in our way of life. In one way the girl on the train had a point. Marriages *are* fragile things. They do break down. It's sensible to realise this. However, it is surely better to enter marriage thinking about avoiding the pitfalls rather than checking on the route to the nearest divorce court. So in this chapter we shall consider some of the pitfalls.

Here are some areas where I've seen marriages come unstuck and in some of these areas my own marriage has been put to the test.

1. STARTING WITHOUT ENOUGH THOUGHT

In a sense this heading could almost cover everything this book is trying to say.

I once moved into a brand-new house. Shortly after moving in, the building contractors finished off the small garden area. They put up the fences and they laid the topsoil. This topsoil was to be the basis of a garden and when it was first put down it looked beautiful. It was a rich, dark brown. It was without any weeds. It looked fine.

But within a short space of time it was a mass of weeds. Now, even allowing for an above-average number of passing birds carelessly dropping seeds on my garden on their way past, there can be only one conclusion. Hidden in that dark brown topsoil, from the very beginning, were the seeds of future trouble. The same can be true of some marriages. They can look fine at the start. The couple can appear to be blissfully in love. But ten years later, on looking back, there is a very different story to tell.

A bit of common sense and careful thought in the days of courtship might have saved a great deal of pain later on. For example, in Appendix A I quote the words of a Building Society executive who speaks of money problems causing marriage breakdowns. Now we live in a topsy-turvy sort of world and there's no way we can forecast some national financial crisis in five years time. We can, however, go into marriage having thought about the sorts of bills that are going to come our way. And if we cannot see how to meet those costs then we can delay the wedding. All this may not quite square with the dreamy love stories in girls' teenage magazines – but then they deal with fiction. In marriages we are dealing with facts.

Another thoughtless start to a marriage is the route of 'making an honest woman' of someone (what a male chauvinistic phrase!). The so-called 'shot-gun' marriage is often a pretty disastrous one (although I can think of some glorious exceptions). Here we need to sort out a few things and look at them clearly. There is the situation where a couple, who are very much committed to each other, have intercourse before marriage and pregnancy results. In this sort of case, especially if the families rally round, probably immediate marriage is the right course. It would surely be a terrible thing if the resultant baby were adopted.

I have heard of some situations, however, where the couple did not marry immediately. The girl kept the baby, helped by her mother. The boy saved, got into a good job and it was altogether a better start when they eventually married. Such cases teach a valuable lesson.

To have rushed in panic into a premature marriage, even though the couple were right for each other, would have been unwise. It would have put immense strains on the couple in the early days of the marriage and that could possibly have led to a later breakdown.

The reason why shocked parents often urge immediate marriage is obvious. They want to make the marriage a sort of cover-up. They want to protect their children from the stigma of having an illegitimate child. But these are short-sighted ways of looking at the problem. They can lead to more pain later on for the couple and their child.

In earlier chapters we have seen that the will of God is for people to be virgins when they marry. Anything other is less than the best. A society which doesn't bother about sex-before-marriage has lost sight of God's values – and this seems to be happening in our times. However, there is one spin-off from our more permissive outlook which is positively good. Society is generally more kind and accepting about children conceived before marriage. There is no need to feel frowned-upon. Marriage needs starting at the right time – otherwise if you start off-balance you can go on and on getting more off-balance until final collapse takes place.

But what about the situation where a baby is conceived as the result of a casual sexual relationship? In such a case a forced marriage is totally wrong. One wrong move does not become any better when another wrong move is added to it. It is far better for the happiness of all concerned for the couple to stay apart and for the baby to be born and adopted. There are thousands of happy married couples longing to adopt. I have very good friends who have been able to thank God for the chance to adopt and for the chance to have been adopted.

And one of them told me how much he thanked God

that nobody was able to persuade his natural parents to have him aborted for 'social reasons'. He has grown up to be a lovely, caring man whose life has been a blessing to hundreds of people.

2. SELF-CENTREDNESS

Marriage asks a great deal of us. It also asks that we live unselfishly for the sake of another person. That is a tall order! If you stand back and look at the history of the human race you will see that the factor that has marred peace on earth more than anything else is human selfishness. The old prophet's words in the Bible (Isaiah 53) were surely on target:

All of us were like sheep that were lost, each of us going his own way ...

We all like to please ourselves. For much of our lives we can stumble along like this but in marriage the crunch comes quickly. Love is about wanting the best for the *other* person. Most of our pop-songs speak of love as if it were a self-centred feeling which is more about *getting* than *giving*. But if two people living under the same roof are only thinking about themselves, then trouble will not be far away.

Sometimes the man wants to keep on all his old habits, friends and activities. He may be a keen sportsman or he may have some time-consuming hobby, and cannot see any problem in leaving his new wife at home in the evenings or at weekends, while he goes off with his friends as he always used to. If the interest is not shared it is selfish behaviour and will cause pain.

On the other hand the girl can also find herself spending large amounts of time away from her husband. Sometimes the mother-daughter relationship is a very close and precious one. In itself, of course, this is fine. The danger, however, is the 'running back to mother' business. It is more than an old comedian's joke. It really does happen and the husband can feel that he takes second place to the wife's family.

Again when it comes to lovemaking, the husband can often be insensitive to the fact that his wife is overtired or at a time in her monthly cycle when she does not feel 'in the mood'. To insist on intercourse would be a very unloving action. It can sometimes happen the other way around when a tired husband who is worried about things at work just cannot feel relaxed enough to make love. A bit of 'tender loving care' is what is needed and jokes about impotence are never jokes.

A crucial time to watch in a marriage is when there are very young children in the home. This means that constant supervision is needed. The degree of dependence of a very young child upon a parent's care is quite awe-inspiring. And so often this is where the husband lets his wife down. This certainly happened with me. I would come home at the end of an interesting day when I had met interesting people. I would find my wife had a meal ready (which was often a near-miraculous achievement on her part!) After tea I would probably do my good deed for the day and wash up, but she would face the bathing and bedding of three very lively children. I might 'help' by walking around issuing orders about 'time for bed now' and sometimes I might read a bed-time story. However, if the phone rang and some friend wanted to see me, the chances were that I would dash off without a thought.

And even when I pulled my weight in getting the family bedded down, I can remember the many times when I would be out for the rest of the evening leaving you-know-who to baby-sit. I can still remember one night when I arrived late from a pleasant evening's chat with a friend to find a very angry and resentful wife.

And I was so surprised that she felt resentful!

In many ways I think my wife complained too little in those early days. If I had only woken up to my selfishness earlier she might have been spared the time, about ten years after we married, when she was hit by nervous exhaustion and became ill.

One thing I learned too late in all this was how much a home with young children can become a prison for the mother. She needs to get out. She needs to meet other people. And the people she needs to meet should include other men! So often the way things work out for young mums is that the only people they see are other young mums.

3. MONEY MATTERS

Another area of self-centredness can be with regard to money. This again is especially true when the wife is coping with the responsibilities of young children and has given up a job of her own. Again, looking back, I can see how I have failed here.

In the latest Church of England wedding service these words are said when the husband gives his bride the wedding ring:

> I give you this ring
> as a sign of our marriage.
> With my body I honour you
> *all that I am I give to you*
> *and all that I have I share with you* ...
> (my italics)

Any salary coming in to the husband is for both partners to the marriage. I don't think it is good enough to think that it is his and that he gives his wife an allowance to cover shopping and a few extras to spend on herself. Of course there are some marriages that handle this the other way around! The husband comes in, hands over his unopened pay packet to the wife, and she takes out some pocket money for him and keeps the rest.

I think the healthy way with money is to see it as belonging to God but given to us to handle carefully on his behalf. That way of thinking soon sorts out what we should spend it on. And it reminds us that giving to needy people and just causes is not 'charity', it is *duty* – and it can be a pretty enjoyable duty as well!

Husbands, beware of expensive hobbies! I thought of asking my wife to say something at this point about my interest in photography but it would probably take another book!

We have touched on the fact that money troubles often wreck marriages. The typical way this can happen is through overcommitting oneself so that in addition to rent or mortgage repayments and all the usual charges, such as gas and electricity, there are also payments on a car, on furniture, on carpets and other items. A social worker once told me that financial over-commitment was often found on housing estates where everyone was trying to 'keep up with' their neighbours.

But who says we have to keep up with anybody? Why not go into marriage with a vow that you will never become a slave to such a stupid set of pressures? There are enough troubles in life outside of our control without adding some that we could avoid.

And beware of so-called 'easy payments'. They nearly always mean bigger sums of money paid out at the end of the day.

Money is a strangely powerful thing. Money matters and bugeting should be talked about openly, and decisions should be shared decisions. If one partner does all this then the other can begin to feel a lesser partner to the marriage.

4. PUTTING THE JOB FIRST

I can think of two or three broken marriages where the job, and the amount of time it demanded, led to the eventual divorce. In one case the husband was working excessive amounts of overtime and the wife also had taken a job so that the family could move to a better home. So it all seemed very worthy. They wanted to give their children the very best. But what happened was that the husband was never home in the evenings and the wife met another, more attentive, man at her place of work. The rot set in pretty quickly after that.

In another case two very talented and ambitious people were pursuing their own careers. They both had good salaries and this led, in turn, to buying a lovely house with superb furnishings. The true cost of this, however, was that they had drifted apart. They had no energy left to work at their own relationship. As a result the husband suddenly announced that he had met and 'fallen in love' with somebody else. They trod the sad route to the divorce court shortly afterwards.

The pressures upon those on the factory floor to put in excessive overtime are often great. The same is true for many in management. Some companies virtually demand of their young executives that the company comes before the family. This cannot be right.

In some extreme cases I would say that marriage and the job will never go together.

There are two similar sorts of situation that can arise.

The first is where the wife's 'job' of mothering her children is put before loving her husband. I have heard of shaky marriages where the husband complained that he felt left out of his wife's affection once the family arrived. Of course there could well be another side to the story. He may have been a self-centred husband who resented having to share his wife with the children. Such things happen. He may not have realised how demanding young children can be upon a mother.

Nevertheless there are many wives who settle for the rôle of 'mum' and turn away from the rôle of 'lover' and even wife. It is as well to see the danger before marriage.

The second variation of the 'job-before-marriage' pitfall is to do with voluntary work. I can think of several broken marriages where this has been one of the factors in the breakdown. It is possible for Christian work (or the voluntary support of other very worthwhile causes) to take up so much time that the marriage gets neglected. I've seen this happen with husbands and with wives, and sometimes with both partners at the same time. Obviously as a Christian I believe we have the most worthwhile message to share. Nor can we leave it at the level of words. God wants Christians to be active and out-going. But one of the things God wants is a happy marriage. Another thing which reflects his will is a cared-for family. If we choose to marry then we must give ourselves to the sort of marriages which reflect God's care and faithfulness.

I love a story that has been told about the famous old evangelist Gipsy Smith. A woman once wrote to him for advice. She told him that she was convinced that the Lord had called her to preach. The problem was that she had a husband and nine children. So what did he advise her to do?

Gipsy Smith's reply was brief. He wrote, 'I am so glad that the Lord has called you to preach. I'm also glad that he has already provided you with a congregation!'

5. SEXUAL HANG-UPS

Marriage counsellors can tell many stories about marriage breakdown where a key factor has been that one or both of the partners has emotional difficulties to do with sexual intercourse. We have discussed some of this in an earlier chapter.

Sexual 'hang-ups', however, can develop later in a marriage. Sometimes frigidity or impotence can develop after years of a fairly normal sexual relationship. The important thing is to admit that something has gone wrong and that expert help is needed. It is surprising how easily some of these problems can be dealt with. But nothing will happen if the person will not admit to needing help. I suppose that many of us are very shy to talk about problems to do with sexual matters, but a doctor is hearing about such things all the time.

But very often we are not only too shy to ask for help from the doctor – *we are too shy or even feel ashamed to discuss the problem with our partners*. This is the sort of thing that ought to have been discovered and put right before the wedding.

An unrealistic approach to family planning is another way in which sexual matters can put a marriage under stress. A couple can begin marriage claiming that 'the Lord will plan our family' or some such pious phrase – or they can simply pretend the problem isn't there. Four years and three babies later there is eviction through unpaid rent, an exhausted wife and a lot of resentment.

The time to get these things sorted out is *before* marriage, and God should never be made the excuse for human irresponsibility. He means us to use our minds and control our affairs. That is why he gave us brains!

6. LACK OF COMMUNICATION

Here is another problem that ought to have been discovered before the wedding bells started ringing.

'Communication' is a big word. It covers talking to each other, but it means far more than this. We can communicate without words. A couple who set out on the lifelong adventure of marriage need to be people who understand each other, know the truth about each other, feel for each other and enjoy listening to each other.

This is why courtship should be about far more than kisses and cuddles. It is about discovering whether the man and the woman really *like* each other and can communicate at other levels than sexually. Indeed sex before marriage can be disastrous for the simple reason that it can distract the couple from discovering the things that could lead to a later breakdown.

Alas, many couples end up as two people living private lives beside each other rather than finding real oneness.

7. FORGETTING OUR HUMANITY

One final area where pitfalls occur is within our own selves as human beings. I am convinced that many husbands and wives end up by having 'affairs' with someone else because they did not remember that they were fallible human beings.

You do not have to be a lustful playboy of a husband to end up in another woman's arms. You just have to be careless. You simply have to forget that women are attractive and often very fond and caring. And you simply have to walk into temptation without realising it.

On several occasions I have seen an affair begin when a man found himself having to help some woman with a genuine need or problem; or the other way around. As the two people got more closely involved, *away from other people*, emotional lines got crossed and they ended up as lovers. The thing to remember is that it could happen to any of us.

I am not suggesting that we do not help members of the opposite sex. I am merely saying that it is very easy for one sort of caring to become another sort of caring. We need to aware of this. And if we spend a great deal of our time alone with someone of the opposite sex the chances of emotional involvement are strong. *There are no exceptions to this rule*. The two may both be Christians. They may both be people of high moral standards. The 'other person' may be a personal friend of the absent wife or husband – but it can still happen.

One of the secrets of keeping a marriage together is recognising how easy it is to break it up. So we need to keep each other closely informed about our movements and who we are meeting and we need to be very aware of our own fallibility. If we drum into ourselves that an affair *could* happen *even to us*, then the chances are that it won't.

And a final word. If in the years ahead something like this ever does happen, do not give up on each other. We have a heavenly Father who does not give up on us and who is always ready to forgive and forget. It is only because of his readiness to forgive that anyone can get anywhere with him.

But our heavenly Father expects us to be like him. A conversation during the life of Jesus makes the point very clearly:

Then Peter came to Jesus and asked, 'Lord, if my brother keeps on sinning against me, how many times do I have to forgive him? Seven times?' 'No, not seven times,' answered Jesus, 'but seventy times seven ...'

Chapter 9

MADE IN HEAVEN?

Marriages – so the saying goes – are made in heaven. I happen to believe that there is truth in the silly old saying. And if it is true that 'someone up there' delights in marriages and married love, then I would suggest that he has an important part to play in keeping the marriage going.

THE MEANING OF LIFE

Many couples find that the sheer wonder of discovering

human love, getting married and starting out on a new life makes them begin to think about God, perhaps for the first time. Certainly the arrival of the first baby is often the time when the most matter-of-fact people begin to ask questions about the meaning of life.

As a Christian I believe that behind everything that exists there is a heavenly Father. This is what Jesus Christ taught and I believe that he is the one who came to show us what God is like. It is difficult to understand or feel for a 'great eternal spirit', but when the character and nature of that eternal spirit is lived out in our world through a human being then we can all see and understand. That is why Jesus is central to discovering what God is like.

But suppose a young couple starting out on life together want to have a Christian marriage, what are the sorts of things that they should do or be? Let me tell a few stories that will show up some of the things that are involved.

TOM AND SALLY

Tom and Sally did not pretend to be 'religious'. Sally would say that she believed in God and Tom would often nod his head when she said that. 'There's probably something in it,' he would agree. 'I mean the Church has been going for centuries and there's been some fantastic people in it. And I still think – you know – there must be some sort of maker behind the world.'

So when Tom and Sally asked for a church wedding it wasn't only because it looked nice in the photographs. There was more to it – not a great deal more, but more all the same. 'We wanted to start it *right*,' was what Sally said. 'Don't ask me what I mean – but you know. Hymns and saying prayers and getting blessed.'

The clergymen who they went to wasn't the greatest, swinging vicar of all time. He was a bit old-fashioned and very coy about the sex side. But Tom and Sally could see that he was a caring man and that God was very real to him. He took the wedding as if it were the most important wedding in his life and Tom and Sally were grateful to him. When they had been kneeling in front of him they had both tried to pray and hoped that they had 'done it right'.

After the honeymoon they moved to a new town development where Tom had found a job. They knew nobody. After three weeks they had a visitor. He was from the local church. The vicar who had married them had written ahead to tell of their arrival. Tom and Sally were embarrassed. They were pleased that someone cared but they didn't see themselves as churchgoing people. They were both out at work and they wanted to keep the weekends to themselves.

However, when Christmas came and the visit to Sally's parents fell through at the last minute, they went to the church for the carol service and they liked it. They were invited to a new year's eve party and said they would think about it. In the end they went and some friendships began.

Before long they were going fairly often. At first it was because they were lonely and they liked the people. But slowly and surely they began to find that the beliefs became their own beliefs. With Sally it was a gradual process but Tom battled against it until one evening, working on his motorbike outside the house, he just 'gave in to God' as he put it.

From that time onwards, and as two daughters arrived on the scene, a Christian home began. Six years later others tell of the naturalness and reality of their Christianity. Tom became a youth leader at the church and probably the only one who could cope with the rougher, tougher kids who came along. Sally was one of those people who was always having others call in for a chat and a 'cuppa'. Their marriage meant more to them and meant more to others. Of course they hit bad patches and had their 'moments'; but they themselves would say that they had a caring heavenly Father and that in some strange way 'Jesus was with them every day'.

For Tom and Sally it wasn't 'going to church' so much as 'belonging to a church'. If we want the best for our marriages then I believe we need to see ourselves and our families as part of the greater family – the family of God's children as seen in a church. I cannot pretend that every church is as welcoming and helpful as the church near Tom and Sally but most of us are within range of a church where God is sincerely worshipped and where people are made to feel that they matter.

ALAN AND TINA

Alan and Tina lived near each other and had done so all their lives. They had first met in the Sunday School of their local church. Over the years they had 'graduated' through the various children's and youth organisations and had formed a good friendship.

Tina started teaching in Sunday School at the age of sixteen and Alan was prominent in the Youth Fellowship. There was a large and cheerful crowd of youngsters in those days and they used to enjoy Christian songs and choruses immensely, with guitars being strummed everywhere. Alan and Tina seemed to be carried along on a tide of happy belief that Jesus Christ was more important than anything and the secret of a happy life. Everyone expected them to get married and they did.

Marriage meant a move of seven miles. Every Sunday

Alan and Tina would get in their Mini and drive back to join their friends at church. After a year or so Tina became pregnant and didn't always feel well. They came back to church less often. They didn't link up locally with a church and after little Robert was born they came back for the Christening. A year later they moved house, this time about a hundred miles north. All links with the home church were gone and somehow, as they looked at 'real life' in the face, the Youth Fellowship days seemed to mean less and less.

For all their church activity and Christian friends Alan and Tina had not discovered God in a personal way. They needed to be carried along by others. When they lost contact with a church they were left with very little to hold on to. If they had linked up, like Tom and Sally, with a church in their new home district it might have been a different story.

Linking up with a church where you live is always the best way. But attending church services and activities is no substitute for finding a personal trust in Jesus Christ as Son of the heavenly Father.

FRANK AND HELEN

Frank and Helen had a great deal in common with Alan and Tina. They had also become members of a thriving church youth group. When their wedding took place the church was packed with praying friends.

But unlike Alan and Tina, Frank and Helen had learnt the importance in their lives of having a daily time of Bible reading and prayer. Helen used to have her 'quiet time' last thing at night when her sister, who shared the bedroom, was usually asleep. Frank, on the other hand, was one of those strange people who are at their best early in the morning! He developed the habit of rising well before breakfast and spending about twenty minutes praying and reading his Bible.

This is not to say that they were great 'saints' or that there were not times when their good habits lapsed. Nevertheless Frank and Helen in their quite ordinary ways were a dedicated Christian couple.

After their marriage they ran into problems. Helen felt strongly that they ought to share their quiet time. As a Christian man and wife surely they should pray together. This led to arguments about the best time. Frank preferred the morning while Helen insisted that it was the worst time in the day as far as she was concerned. Again Frank felt he needed a personal time for prayer and the sort of Bible study that he liked did not seem to interest Helen half as much.

It may sound crazy but this issue nearly ruined their marriage. Looking back it is almost laughable, but at the time it seemed to cast gloom over everything for days on end.

Fortunately things began to get sorted out when Helen broke down and blurted it all out to one of the members at their new church. She and her husband invited Frank and Helen for a meal at their home and the two couples talked over the whole issue.

What Frank and Helen had to learn was that while a Christian couple should indeed be able to pray together, there was no need to insist that all their praying and Bible reading had to be a joint activity. In marriage we create a oneness but we still remain two people who are loved by God as individuals. We need to find a devotional life that does justice to both sides – the oneness and the two individuals.

Many Christian couples I know have a simple time of prayer together every day, but also have their separate individual times when they try to be quiet before God.

What Frank and Helen began to do made a great deal of sense. Frank continued to get up bright and early and would pray and read the Bible in the kitchen before making a start on breakfast.

At breakfast they would take turns to read from a book of selections from the Bible and one or the other would lead in a brief prayer for the events of the day to come. Until she stopped work to have her first baby Helen used to go up to the bedroom a little while before Frank and read and pray in bed. After they had started their family she found the time following lunch, when young Simon was having a nap, was an ideal time to relax and think and read and pray.

The important thing is to find a simple pattern that allows both of you to have a time of quiet and also makes room for developing the habits of prayer together. My wife and I like to start and end the day with a short prayer and (in the morning) a reading from the Bible or from a book of selected Bible readings such as *Every Day*[1] or *Daily Light*[2]. Apart from that we have our own ways of reading the Bible and praying.

JOHN AND SUSAN

Everyone who knew them said that John was brilliant and would go to the top. He had become an active Christian at University where he had also met Susan. They married two years after they both left.

They were determined to set up a Christian home. They got themselves involved with a flourishing church and it was not long before John was one of its leading members. They prayed regularly and when their first child arrived they prayed with her from the very day she

[1] Published by Scripture Union
[2] Published by Samuel Bagster

was born. 'I believe there should never be a day when she hasn't been made aware of God,' Susan would say.

John was moved by his oil company. The links forged with the church in the new area were less secure. John was now becoming a globe-trotter and moving up the promotion ladder at great speed. The number of children grew to three and they moved again to a larger house and to the sort of property that was 'more appropriate to John's position in life'.

The social life of the couple changed. Susan was much involved in the local tennis club and when John was home, they entertained their new friends and John's business associates in grand style. After a couple of years they moved again to a larger house. John was now the managing director.

There is no need for prosperity and success to have this sort of effect, but it did in the case of John and Susan. As they grew more prosperous and as John was more and more busy, God was squeezed out. There was no moment when John and Susan stopped believing. What happened was that their Christian beliefs became less and less important. They continued to go to their local church at least once a month but prayer was less and less a part of their lives.

I've met quite a few people like John and Susan. They were not always as successful or wealthy, but they became busy and so interested in material possessions that their Christianity shrank almost to nothing. As their faith shrank so, in many cases, did their happiness and peace. Often their values became other than Christian. Their children grew without any of the benefits of a Christian home.

It can happen to any of us and the best way to avoid it happening is to be prepared in advance. I'm sure that God gives some of us the talents and abilities to be successful and I am sure we are meant to use them. But the top priority is to serve God with one's life and not to serve money or fame or popularity or whatever else may become a rival.

There is a strange verse in the Bible in which Jesus is pictured on the outside of a house which is full of people who need him.

'Listen! I stand at the door and knock; if anyone hears my voice and opens the door, I will come into his house and eat with him, and he will eat with me.'
Revelation 3: 20

It is a powerful picture. It is all too easy to leave Jesus Christ out of our personal lives and our married lives. Even when we say that we believe in him, it is easy to be so busy with other things that we do not stop to be still before him or to ask ourselves whether we are doing what he wants. I believe that there is a sense in which Jesus can actually come into our lives. The Bible speaks of the Holy Spirit of God. It states that the Spirit brings Jesus-like qualities into our behaviour and makes us aware of the heavenly Father.

Marriage is the greatest adventure of all. Two people set out to share their lives in a total way and to stick together in the bad times as well as the good. I believe we need all the help that God can give us and God believes the same! That is why the Holy Spirit of Jesus is waiting to be allowed into everyone's heart and everyone's home.

Let him come in!

TEN BASIC GUIDELINES FOR A CHRISTIAN HOME

1. Belong to a church.

2. Start and end the day with a simple prayer.
3. Make Bible reading and personal prayer a part of your life.
4. Never go to bed angry with another member of the family. First make peace.
5. Welcome others into your home.
6. Pray with your children from the day they are born.
7. Share your problems with each other and never be afraid to seek the help of others.
8. The husband should be the leader but his leadership must help each member to be fulfilled and happy.
9. Work away at loving your neighbour.
10. Never forget that God loves the world and wants his people to pass on his love.

Appendix A

A ROOF OVER OUR HEADS

Once upon a time, I suppose, the young bridegroom dashed off and built a hut or a wigwam or dug a cosy cave to which he could take his lovely young bride. Nowadays it is far more complicated!

When you get back from your honeymoon (assuming you can afford one) you will need somewhere to live. This is no small matter. 'Love' will not 'conquer all' in such things, in spite of what the pop songs may say. It needs some hard thinking, a great deal of searching through the small ads plus a good bit of leg-work.

At this point two big decisions need to be faced.

1. SHOULD WE WAIT?

In the days when our fathers and grandfathers were young, people seem to have married later in life. People often waited until their late twenties before naming the day. The point was that it gave them more time to save and put a home together. Today teenage brides and grooms abound. We marry younger and start with less in the bank and call it 'romantic'. I have a feeling the oldies knew a thing or two.

They may have waited too long, but I am quite sure that many today do not wait long enough. As a result many couples marry without the sort of accommodation that would give them a good start in life. Tensions develop and if the couple have a baby too soon hardship and even separation can follow. And at the end of the story there is more work for the divorce courts. I know this sounds gloomy – but it happens to be true in far too many cases.

So what I am asking is this – would it be better for your marriage to wait a year or two? You still have each other. You will have the joy of planning and saving for your home. If a couple of years could make all the difference then the wait will prove its worth over the next half-century! Think about it!

2. SHOULD WE MOVE?

It is often the case that house prices and rentals are far better in some other part of the country. If you were prepared to move you would have a better home of your own far sooner.

In such a case there are two things to bear in mind. The first is the matter of careers. This is especially important in the case of the husband because, when children come, he will probably have to be sole breadwinner. However, in these days when two lots of earnings are usually needed to get a home started, the job prospects for the wife are also pretty important.

So we must ask—will moving help or hinder career and job prospects? People sometimes move hoping that something will turn up. That is not good enough. To start married life living on the dole is no way to begin. It is no shame if it was not your fault. But I feel it is wrong to deliberately bring about such a situation. So often a girl can get a job quicker than the fellow and that can prove a humiliating experience for the new head of the new home. He can feel his manhood is being taken away.

It certainly would be wrong to marry and move if that meant that the man had to give up some course of study or training or his place in a promotion list. A wife is meant to make her husband more of what he ought to be, not less.

The second thing to bear in mind when thinking about moving is whether you are prepared to leave your friends and all the associations of the past. You will notice that I have not mentioned the matter of leaving one's parents. This is because *marriage means leaving one's parents*. In the Bible's creation account we have already come across the words: '... a man leaves his father and mother and is united with his wife, and they become one.' Leaving one's parents is part of the meaning of getting married and if a person is not prepared for that, then he or she is not prepared for marriage.

This is not to say that one *deserts* one's parents. Of course not. We do not stop loving our parents because we have married. But we do stop living in their home, because we have set up a new home.

But parents are not the only people we love. We have friends with whom we may have grown up, and we can be deeply in love with the old familiar sights of our neighbourhood. To leave and move to an unknown district and to where you do not know anyone is a big step. You can end up feeling very lonely – especially in a new house on a brand new housing estate where nobody knows each other and there is no sense of community.

Having said all this, if you are young and willing to be outgoing you can help make a community. It is easier to make friends when you are young. If you are both still working in the earlier days of your marriage you may well find friends at your places of work. When a family is started, children have a habit of playing with other children and breaking down barriers (and a few other things!). And before children come you may well find local clubs, hobbies groups or evening classes where you can make friends.

Here is where it is such a joy to be a Christian in a country like ours. You belong to another and bigger family and you are seldom very far from a church where there is some genuine fellowship.

The thing we have to remember in all this is that life is all about change. If we do not move, our friends probably will! The neighbourhood we love will have a dual-carriageway pushed through it, or the familiar streets will be devastated to make way for a multi-storey car park and shopping centre. The only permanent features of life are God and the fact that the world is full of other people.

LIVING WITH IN-LAWS

I have already said that marriage is about leaving one's parents. In spite of this many young couples start their married lives in the home of one or the other's parents. Should this never happen or are there some guidelines?

It can, in fact, work out quite successfully as long as some things are realised *on all sides* from the start.

First, the married couple must be seen to have left their parents. This will not happen if they are living as members of the family. They need to have part of the house to themselves which is out of bounds to the parents unless they are invited. They need to have more than a bedroom. They need, at least, a bed-sit and a kitchen of their own. It has often been said that women can share a bathroom but it is asking too much to expect them to share a kitchen! I agree.

Second, the arrangement should not be for a long time. Anything longer than a year is what I would call a long time. As long as there is a date to work towards this can be a tolerable, even happy, arrangement. After that, real tensions can set in. We are all imperfect people and it shows at times like these. For the parents there is the strain of not having the use of the whole of the house. For the young couple there is the feeling of having their new 'style' cramped (in every sense). No – we may all love each other, but we need room to feel free to be ourselves.

LIVING IN FURNISHED ROOMS

Many young couples start out together in furnished rooms paying rental to a landlord or landlady.

In this sort of arrangement one has to consider some basically human issues. So often the couple are living in someone else's house with the minimum of reconstruction. It may be called a 'flat' but it rarely seems like it! Once again we need to be clear about what is exclusive to the couple and what has to be shared. As we saw earlier, sharing kitchens does not work. If that is part of the deal, say 'no'. At the end of the day a postponed wedding is far better than a strained one.

Again landladies tend to have definite views about music. Loud hi-fi pop is almost never appreciated. This is not a little matter – it means that you must keep the volume down or you get out.

Another area where there can be tension is the matter of having friends in and holding parties. I think it is unreasonable to rent out rooms and expect people to live like hermits, but landlords often have the whip hand. Yet if you look at it from their point-of-view you can see their anxieties. They have rented out a couple of rooms but they do not want to feel they are being taken over or crowded out! Some older people find a large group of boisterous young adults daunting and even frightening.

In all this the secret of any successful relationship is to set out to be caring and considerate. Landlords and landladies are *people* too! They have their fears and anxieties. Some of them do not really want to rent out part of their houses but feel they have been forced to through economic circumstances. It makes all the difference to them to feel they can trust their tenants and to sense that the young couple upstairs care about them.

I know of several cases where lifelong friendships have been started between a couple and the people from whom they rented rooms. If the relationship turns out to be at a formal level, make sure that this is because the landlord wants it that way. Always try to be a friend – it is a good rule for life.

One final matter. The whole point of living in rooms, whether with in-laws or with someone else, *is so that you can save*. If the level of rent is such that both your salaries are needed to make ends meet, you will end up trapped in that sort of accommodation. This means that having children has to be delayed and that any 'mistakes' in this direction can end with eviction. Before you go ahead you need to work out your sums realistically.

RENTING AN UNFURNISHED FLAT

This is a much better arrangement than living in furnished rooms. It angers me that we do not have nearly enough rented accommodation in this country.

I am assuming that we are talking about a self-contained, purpose-built or properly-converted flat. You take possession of it bare and empty and you are able to create your own 'style' upon it with your own furniture and curtains and all the rest.

Once again, however, there needs to be some clear thinking. Money going out in rental is not the same as money paying off a mortgage on your own home. In other countries many people live all their lives in rented accommodation, moving from one type to another as family size dictates. In our daft little island we are positively neurotic about owning houses and on the other hand are used to a situation where most rented accommodation is controlled by the local authority and where one needs to qualify and to be on a council housing list. It is often left to new town developers to show the way with private but rented homes.

If you were to start life together by renting a flat would that mean you were unable to save to buy a property? It needs to be thought over carefully. In some areas there are imaginative rental-purchase schemes where you can end up owning what you started by renting. This usually applies to houses rather than flats. Keep your eyes open.

HOUSING ASSOCIATIONS

A fairly recent healthy development in the British housing scene is the Housing Association. By this means, homes for renting are made available throughout the country especially in areas of greatest housing need. The Housing Association works very closely with the local authority.

Housing Associations not only build new properties, they also do a fine work in renovating older premises and making them into purpose-built units of housing. Rents are set on the 'fair rent' basis by the local Rent Officer.

(In Appendix C you will find a list of the regional offices of the Housing Corporation. They can send details of any Housing Societies in the area where you are hoping to live. The local Housing Aid Centre will also be able to help with details.)

CO-OWNERSHIP

In response to the ever-increasing price of housing, various new ideas in housing associations have arisen, such as co-ownership. There are co-ownership schemes all over England, Scotland and Wales and one can find out more details by writing to:

The Council of Co-ownership Housing Societies,
11a Quickthorn Close,
Whitchurch,
Bristol, BS14 0RG.

(Letters should enclose a stamped addressed envelope.)

Co-ownership schemes are unusual in that one becomes both a tenant and a joint owner of a property! The tenants pay a rent with one month's rent paid in advance. There is usually a returnable deposit to pay in advance which often works out around three months' rent.

In many ways the arrangement works like a renting agreement. However, when you leave to move somewhere else you are entitled to a premium if you have lived in the house or flat for at least five years. This means that you get a share in the increased value of the property. If the value of the property decreases there is no need to panic – you do not have to pay anything but obviously there is no premium.

Unfortunately these imaginative schemes tend to have long waiting lists but there is no harm in making enquiries.

BUYING YOUR OWN PLACE

This is the dream of many young couples. I will say

little about it here simply because there is so much to say. Your nearest bookshop will almost certainly stock one or two practical paperback books on the subject. Some banks and Building Societies (see Appendix B) also have helpful pamphlets and booklets.

Let me simply say that this is an area where you need proper advice. You will need the services of a solicitor. You will almost certainly need to borrow money which has to be paid back with interest and you will almost certainly need to stump up a deposit from your own savings – usually about ten per cent of the purchase price of the property.

Everybody is very fussy when a house is being bought. Solicitors want to check that the land does not belong to someone else who will claim it back in two months' time! There have to be 'searches' made. And Building Societies will insist on surveyor's reports to make sure the house is not falling apart on top of an underground cave. It is all very frustrating but rather necessary. If you are going to put all your money into a house, you cannot afford anything going wrong later on, leaving you with a crumbling or worthless piece of property.

'STARTER HOMES'

Some local authorities have pioneered the idea of 'Starter Homes'. These are purpose-built houses for first-time buyers which are soundly built but are sold in an un-decorated state and without the extras of kitchen units and so on.

The prices are extremely attractive by present-day standards and there is usually clever planning to allow for garages and extensions to be added by the house-owner at a later date. Because they are new properties

Building Societies will usually offer high-percentage mortgages which means that the buyer's own deposit is kept to a minimum.

It is worth checking whether your local authority does this sort of thing.

COUNCIL HOUSES

It is always worth finding out what the local situation is in terms of the availability of council houses and flats. Local authorities vary in what they have to offer and in how they set about allocating their property.

Your local council will have a Housing Department and this in turn will have an allocation office. Usually councils concentrate on trying to house families and many operate a system which awards points according to the needs of the families on their waiting lists. Newlyweds are likely to figure low on such lists as a result.

Nevertheless some councils are anxious to keep young couples in their areas and provide a certain amount of property to encourage this. Some new and developing towns try to attract new residents through offering immediately available accommodation.

WORTHWHILE

Getting a roof over your heads is no easy matter and a chapter like this may seem depressing and overpowering. At the end of the day, however, we are talking about setting up a new home and few things in life are more worthwhile than that.

Appendix B

MARRIAGES COST MONEY

I was talking to a Building Society executive one day. The subject had got around to broken marriages. 'We're finding a growing number of home loans going sour on us through marriage breakdown,' he said.

'And the thing that breaks many of them up is money. They overcommit themselves. They get into debt, and things just fall apart.'

One of the things I am anxious to say as clearly as possible in this book, is that marriage needs a realistic approach. Starry-eyed romantics are heading for trouble. One of the realities of life is that things cost money. Quite apart from putting together the fittings and furnishings of a home the week-by-week running expenses are surprisingly high.

WHERE THE MONEY GOES

Let's remind ourselves of what happens to the pay packet or salary:

1. The taxman gets his cut!
2. There are national health insurance and pension contributions.
3. There might be union dues.
4. We have fares to and from work.
5. There are rent or home loan repayments.
6. We have rates and water rates to pay.
7. There are gas and electricity bills.
8. There may be telephone bills.
9. We need clothes and shoes.

10. We have toilet requirements.
11. There is a large bill for our food.
12. We have clothes-washing costs.
13. We may be running a car or motor-bike.

And on top of all these is the money we spend on entertainment, holidays, hobbies, plus any money we plan to give away. So all in all life costs a great deal of money and marriage doesn't change a thing in that respect. Indeed, if we have been living with parents, it is almost certain that marriage will mean that life becomes more expensive.

A FAMILY BUDGET

A good habit to develop from the start of a marriage is that of keeping a family budget. Quite simply this means working out how much money is coming in to the home and planning how it should be spent.

Many of us are very casual with our money. As a result we thoughtlessly spend a pound here and a few pounds there week after week. It all mounts up and we find ourselves stacked with non-essentials and short of the cash to buy something we really need. A family budget helps create the sort of attitude to money that makes sure it is being used for the right things.

ONE OR TWO SALARIES?

Of course it could be argued against all this that in these days the girl usually carries on working and therefore we have two lots of earnings coming into the house. That may be true, but we need to put up a couple of warning lights here.

Let us imagine a newly married couple living in rented

accommodation. They both have good jobs with good salaries. They can afford overseas holidays every year and they run a new car. It looks as if everything is going well for them but the truth is that they are living in a fool's paradise. What's wrong is that they are not saving. Rent is going out on accommodation which will prove unsuitable when they want to start a family.

And this leads to the second story. Let us imagine another young couple. They are buying a house, unlike the first couple. They run a battered old car which they maintain themselves. They too are both earning but they are using all of both salaries merely to pay their way. What will happen if they want to start a family and the girl has to give up her job?

In those early months of marriage when both husband and wife are out at work *it is absolutely vital that some saving is going on.* It is important to set yourselves a standard of living that is realistic and will allow a family to be started after two or three years or so. To plan to wait much longer is not a good thing. It would probably be better to delay marriage. Of course, after getting married, things might crop up that made the delaying of children a sensible thing – but that is another matter.

Marriage is a life-long business and needs to be 'paced'. The early stages are all about patiently building a base for more adventurousness later on. So often we think of it the other way around. We think of the early days as times of 'married bliss' or 'one long honeymoon' and then as the years go by family responsibilities grow and the finances get tight it becomes drudgery. I can think of plenty of marriages where this drudgery is all too obvious, and very often it could have been avoided if the couple had saved more and been wiser with their money in the early years.

A BANK ACCOUNT

I still meet people who try to save by putting money under the floorboards! I know of some older people who do not feel safe unless their wallets are full or their handbags are stuffed with pound notes. It is a foolish way of handling money.

Years ago during the 1939–45 war a bomb fell near a house in a part of Essex I know. The next day people began picking up pound notes all over the place – children could not believe their eyes! What had happened was that the roof had been blown off the house and in the attic of that house the owner had hoarded a small fortune – in biscuit tins. He was convinced it would be safer there than in a bank.

But it wasn't.

So if you haven't done it yet – start a bank account. Go to the local branch of a reputable bank with branches throughout the country, go up to a cashier and simply say: 'Could you tell me how to open an account please?' He or she will probably ask you to wait for a moment and get you to speak to someone like the assistant manager. In a very few moments the deed can be done.

You can open an account with a first deposit of a very small amount. You fill up a pay slip and hand it over. You will be equipped with a book of blank cheques which are the main means of drawing cash and making payments. It is worth asking for a cheque card which is a sort of simple identity card bearing an example of your signature. The bank may not issue such a card immediately, so in the early days of using cheques it is important to have some means of identification on you such as a driving licence.

For some reason many people feel that there could be embarrassing questionnaires or that banks are only interested in the very wealthy. The truth is that most of those with bank accounts are as poor as you are! Banks, believe it or not, are always anxious to have new customers.

After the wedding day it is best to alter the account into a joint account in the names of both husband and wife. This is a tidier and more trustful way of doing things. Another sensible thing to do is to have two different accounts at the bank. All you have to do is to ask! I do this and I pay a fixed amount every month (by what the bank calls a 'standing order') from my number 1 account into my number 2. This second account is the one I use to pay my gas, electricity and telephone bills, plus an annual life assurance premium. I have worked out what it is likely to add up to, divided it by twelve and arranged to pay it in monthly instalments from one account to the other. It makes my monthly salary a bit smaller but it means that I am not knocked sideways when the bills come in. Every bank has a selection of leaflets which set out all the basic things they can do to help you run your money matters sensibly. And using a cheque book is more sensible than having a pocket full of banknotes.

Those who are paid monthly can ask their employers for the money to be paid straight into the bank. Those who are paid by a pay packet can simply keep what they think they will need for the week and pay in at the local branch of any bank anything that is left over. All the major banks have a system of seeing that what is paid in anywhere is paid over to your account very quickly. Computers are marvellous things!

(Those normally paid weekly in a pay packet can always ask if their pay can go straight into their bank account. Many employers actually prefer this.)

BEWARE OF CREDIT CARDS

Most banks offer a credit card system which is a very handy idea but one that can lead to a great deal of trouble later on. Some department stores and other shops also have their own credit cards. Basically a credit card is a 'buy now pay later' system. I find it very useful to buy my petrol on a credit card and pay at the end of the month. I sometimes buy clothes on a credit card and make 'never never' payments for a few months until the debt is cleared. This is fine but the danger is that we can forget that credit cards are all about *owing money*. Some people just cannot handle credit cards. They buy what they cannot afford and find that they owe too much money to the bank which operates the scheme. On top of this they will be charged interest every month.

From a bank's point of view a credit card scheme is a way of making profit. They are 'selling' you money. They get interest on what they loan you. It's fair enough as long as we know the rules of the game – but know the rules we must!

BORROWING FROM THE BANK

While credit cards need watching, banks have other ways of lending money. One of the advantages of getting a loan from your bank is that you have to talk it over with a bank official. This is good. The bank usually *wants* to make loans because it charges interest and makes money out of the exercise. So it is 'on your side'. On the other hand the bank has to be confident that you and I can repay our loans. What comes out of all this is a sensible check on our spending plans.

That is why I feel borrowing from the bank is always better than *hire purchase*. Many young people get themselves in dreadful trouble from taking on too much hire purchase. Applying for bank loans to purchase the same items might have led to a friendly refusal which could have saved a later disaster. Borrowing is a dangerous business. Sometimes we have to do it and when those times come we should get the best advice possible.

SAVING MONEY

Banks are also willing to pay you interest as well as charge it. You can ask about deposit accounts where you arrange for a sum of money to be left with the bank for a guaranteed minimum amount of time.

Another way of saving is to buy British Savings Bonds from your bank or post office. These have to be bought in multiples of £5. They earn you interest at a very good rate and can be cashed at a month's notice. If you hold on to your bonds for five years you receive a higher rate of interest.

The National Savings Bank and the National Giro-bank at the Post Office or a Trustee Savings Bank are other ways of saving and well worth visiting to pick up the free literature. If, like me, you get easily confused with the 'official' language of such pamphlets never be afraid to ask for advice. The National Savings Bank also offers National Savings Certificates (which can also be bought through any bank). These are a good way of saving. They grow in value over a four-year period and as no tax has to be paid on the greater value they offer the equivalent of a very high rate of interest.

BUILDING SOCIETIES

Probably the wisest form of saving for those about to get married is through a Building Society. It may be that at some stage in the future you will need a loan (often called, mistakenly, a mortgage). The Building Societies serve two sets of people, their investors and their borrowers. When it comes to granting a loan for house-buying, a Building Society always gives preference to one of its investors, and if you have been saving with a Building Society, you are one of its investors. If a young couple get engaged and discover they are saving through two different Societies it is probably wisest to put both your accounts (separately) with one or the other. Before doing that it makes sense to see whether one or the other offers slightly better terms.

Some Societies offer slightly better interest rates to investors but these are often offset by higher interest rates to their borrowers. If you expect to be a borrower in the near future it is worth remembering this!

GOOD ADVICE

Some newspapers have regular features to help those saving their money. The situation is constantly changing. Once again one's bank manager can prove a valuable adviser.

LIFE ASSURANCE

Another form of saving is taking out an endowment policy with a Life Assurance Company. There are so many of these companies around that it is wise to consult your bank manager for advice. He would certainly warn you off any doubtful company but probably point out that the 'big names' deserve to be big and are thoroughly trustworthy. However, different companies have slightly different things built into their policies and it is worth shopping around.

Some people think life assurance is a pretty gloomy subject. The do not want to think of dying so they don't do anything about it. But life assurance is far more than saving money for someone else when you die, it is a very good way of saving for your later years. Life can be hard for pensioners and every bit of help for such times is common sense.

A friend of mine sells life assurance. She is a keen Christian and when she was considering going into this form of work she asked the minister of her church: 'Do you think I should do this sort of work as a Christian?'

'Yes,' he replied. 'I think it is a very Christian sort of work to do. You are helping people to do a very Christian thing.' Having said this he opened his Bible and showed her a verse of scripture. Here is what she read:

> But if anyone does not take care of his relatives, especially the members of his own family, he has denied the faith and is worse than an unbeliever.
>
> 1 Timothy 5:8

Buying life assurance like all sensible handling of money in your married life, is one way of showing that you love each other. Foolishness in these matters nearly always brings unhappiness.

Your marriage must be too important to allow such foolishness.

Appendix C

HOUSING CORPORATION OFFICES

Headquarters
149 Tottenham Court Road, London W1P 0BN Telephone 01 387 9466

London and Home Counties (North)
Waverley House, 7–12 Noel Street, London W1V 3PB Telephone 01 434 2161

London and Home Counties (South)
Pembroke House, Wellesley Road, Croydon, Surrey CR9 2BR Telephone 01 681 3771

Wales
24 Cathedral Road, Cardiff CF1 9LJ Telephone 0222 384611

West
35a Guildhall Centre, Exeter, EX4 3HL Telephone 0392 51052/4

West Midlands
Norwich Union House, Waterloo Road, Wolverhampton WV1 4BP Telephone 0902 24654

East Midlands
Phoenix House, 16 New Walk, Leicester LE1 6TF Telephone 0533 546762

North-West
Elisabeth House, 16 St Peters Square, Manchester M2 3DF Telephone 061 228 2951

Merseyside
6th Floor, Corn Exchange Buildings, Fenwick Street,
Liverpool L2 7RD   Telephone 051 236 0406

North-East
St Paul's House, 23 Park Square South, Leeds LS1 2ND
Telephone 0532 46960

East North & South Scotland
Forth House, 13–17 Forth Street, Edinburgh EH1 3LE
Telephone 031 557 2300

Strathclyde
5th Floor, Mercantile Chambers, 53 Bothwell Street,
Glasgow G2 6TS   Telephone 041 226 6411

Scottish Head Office
19 Coates Crescent, Edinburgh EH3 7AF   Telephone
031 226 3153

Appendix D

WHOM YOU CAN AND CANNOT MARRY

(a) The Marriage Acts of 1907 and 1921 allow a man's marriage to his deceased wife's sister, deceased brother's widow, deceased wife's brother's daughter, deceased wife's sister's daughter, father's deceased brother's widow, mother's deceased brother's widow, deceased wife's father's sister, deceased wife's mother's sister, brother's deceased son's widow and sister's deceased son's widow.

(b) The Book of Common Prayer of the Church of England states:

A man may not marry his
mother, daughter, father's mother, mother's mother, son's daughter, daughter's daughter, sister, father's daughter, mother's daughter, wife's mother, wife's daughter, father's wife, son's wife, father's father's wife, mother's father's wife, wife's father's mother, wife's mother's mother, wife's son's daughter, wife's daughter's daughter, son's son's wife, daughter's son's wife, father's sister, mother's sister, brother's daughter or sister's daughter.

A woman may not marry her
father, son, father's father, mother's father, son's son, daughter's son, brother, father's son, mother's son, husband's father, husband's son, mother's husband, daughter's husband, father's mother's husband, mother's mother's husband, husband's

father's father, husband's mother's father, husband's son's son, husband's daughter's son, son's daughter's husband, daughter's daughter's husband, father's brother, mother's brother, brother's son or sister's son.

Hodder Christian Paperbacks

HAPPY FAMILIES

Jean Watson

How to bring up children God's way.

What is a good Christian upbringing? Jean Watson has addressed herself to this vital question, searched the Bible and asked the opinions of over thirty other families. What do you do when your child throws a tantrum? How can you build confidence in children? What about teenage rebellion?

In an age when children are exposed to an increasingly worldly and frightening society, Jean Watson offers timely and welcome advice. It is rooted in her own family and Christian experience, and combines sound common sense with biblical principle. The material is carefully divided under subheadings for easy reference, and relates to children at every age and stage.

Jean Watson is editor of *Through the Year with David Watson*, and has written for BBC's Play School.

LET ME BE A WOMAN

Elisabeth Elliot

'*The love of a woman and a man gains immeasurably in power when placed under divine restraint . . .*'

Elisabeth Elliot is one of Christendom's most able writers. Here she couples her own observations with careful, life-long study of the Bible to produce a balanced presentation on womanhood. This book is her gift to the daughter whose father, Jim Elliot, was martyred by Auca Indians in 1956. Now Valerie is a young woman, on the threshold of marriage and the establishment of her own home.

Centred primarily on Christian marriage, this book examines male-female relationships in a series of penetrating essays.

Elisabeth Elliot is author of many books including *No Graven Image* and *Through Gates of Splendour*.

STRAIGHT TALK TO MEN AND THEIR WIVES

James Dobson

For every husband who wants to know what it means to be a man. A warm, intensely personal book on family relationships.

'If families are to survive the incredible stresses and dangers they now face, it will be because husbands and fathers provide loving leaderships in their homes, placing their wives and children at the highest level on their system of priorities,' claims Dr Dobson.

In response to the aching need he has heard expressed by both men and women, Dr Dobson offers a bold re-definition of what it means to be a man. How should a man relate to his wife and children; his work and money; his masculinity and emotions; his mortality and his God?

Books abound on the nature and role of women. *Straight Talk to Men and their Wives* redresses the balance: a sane, thinking, often witty contribution to enrich family life.

Dr Dobson is Associate Clinical Professor of Pediatrics at the University of California School of Medicine, and a widely recognised counsellor on family questions.